Judith S. Eaton

STRENGTHENING
COLLEGIATE
EDUCATION
in
COMMUNITY
COLLEGES

Jossey-Bass Publishers · San Francisco

Substantial discounts on bulk quantities of Jossey-Bass books are available to corporations, professional associations, and other organizations. For details and discount information, contact the special sales department at Jossey-Bass Inc., Publishers. (415) 433-1740; Fax (415) 433-0499.

For sales outside the United States, contact Maxwell Macmillan International Publishing Group, 866 Third Avenue, New York, New York 10022.

Manufactured in the United States of America. Nearly all Jossey-Bass books, jackets, and periodicals are printed on recycled paper that contains at least 50 percent recycled waste, including 10 percent postconsumer waste. Many of our materials are also printed with vegetable-based ink; during the printing process these inks emit fewer volatile organic compounds (VOCs) than petroleum-based inks. VOCs contribute to the formation of smog.

Library of Congress Cataloging-in-Publication Data

Eaton, Judith S.
    Strengthening collegiate education in community colleges / Judith S. Eaton.
        p. cm. — (Jossey-Bass higher and adult education series)
    Includes bibliographical references and index.
    ISBN 1-55542-615-8
    1. Community colleges — United States. 2. Education, Higher — United States — Aims and objectives. I. Title. II. Series.
LB2328.15.U6E28   1994
378'.052'0973 — dc20
                                                  93-46056
                                                              CIP

FIRST EDITION
HB Printing   10 9 8 7 6 5 4 3 2 1   *Code 9410*

A publication in
The Jossey-Bass
Higher and Adult Education Series

Consulting Editor
Community Colleges

Arthur M. Cohen
University of California, Los Angeles

Contents

Preface

The community college has been the nation's primary site of access to higher education. More students have enrolled in community colleges than in any other sector of American higher education. The enormous enrollment growth in the higher education enterprise, to which Americans frequently point with pride, could not have occurred without the community college. Central to occupying this important position was the community college's investment in its collegiate role: providing transferable liberal arts and career education.

Over time, however, the community college has drifted away from its higher education emphasis and, simultaneously, has redefined its commitment to access. Access remains pivotal in community college thinking, but commitment to it has become increasingly diffuse, undermining the community college role as the key entry point to higher education. What was initially intended as access to lower-division, college-level education that led to the baccalaureate degree became, instead, access to a range of educational and quasi-educational programs and services, many of which were not at the college level and were not accompanied by the baccalaureate as an educational goal. By allowing this to happen, the community college shifted from a crucial site of higher education opportunity to an ambiguous site of quasi-educational opportunity.

How did this happen? In retrospect, we can point to several key times in the history of the educational role of the community college during which its collegiate role was clearly being devalued. First, the two-year college that emerged from World War II was an institution that was unwilling to invest as much in its liberal arts and transfer efforts as it had in earlier years. The shift from the designation *junior* to that of *community* was a powerful signal confirming that the traditional collegiate role of the two-year college was becoming less important and that a vocational and community-based role was to receive significant emphasis.

Second, by the early 1970s, the shift in orientation had borne fruit. Enrollments in the liberal arts had declined from as many as 75 percent of all students in community colleges to approximately 50 percent, and transfer activity had declined from 60 percent of students to no more than 25 percent.

Third, by the mid 1980s, additional repercussions from this shift were being seen. Community college educators were able to document attenuation of the collegiate emphasis by the fact that students in college-level courses were being asked to do less and less work and the academic demands made on them were being seriously diluted.

Why did this happen? One reason was indifference on the part of leadership. During these years of deterioration of the collegiate role, national community college leaders did not place a premium on the collegiate function and access to the baccalaureate. Instead, they emphasized the other purposes of the community college; this, in turn, meant that the collegiate function was not the focus of their creative attention and investment of energy.

A second reason was the faculty's reaction to student capabilities. The student population served by the community college grew less and less prepared for college-level work, and faculty responded with classroom fare that was less demanding in both quality and quantity. However plausible this action appeared at the time, it weakened the academic environment.

A third reason was a change in the climate in which the community college operated. These were years of increasingly vocational interests on the part of students, a growing paraprofessional job market, and greater availability of federal, state, and corporate funds for vocational training. They were years when community colleges grappled with issues such as racial and gender equity and the need to provide social services such as child care. These interests and issues made tremendous demands on the community college to provide more education and services than were included in the liberal arts and transfer functions.

Audience and Scope of the Book

How can the community college restore its commitment to the collegiate function? This is the critical question addressed here. The book is a call to community college faculty, administrators, and trustees to make a major investment in the collegiate purpose of their institutions. *Strengthening Collegiate Education in Community Colleges* challenges both today's scholars of the community college and their students—the scholars of tomorrow. Its audiences also include elected and appointed policy makers and all those whose decisions affect some part of the future of the community college.

Overview of the Contents

The book attempts to provide a strong conceptual and practical foundation for vigorous renewal of the collegiate community college. Chapter One provides an overview of the community college as a collegiate institution, using a four-part definition of what *collegiate* means. The chapter asks whether or not the community college should be collegiate, questions whether it can be collegiate, and directly addresses the implications of strengthening the collegiate purpose. It then identifies the assumptions on which the book's discussion of the collegiate community college is based.

Chapter Two describes the history of the educational role of the community college as it evolved from the junior college of the early twentieth century. Chapter Three examines the contemporary context of the community college—the competing visions of the institution's friends and the major concerns of its critics.

Chapter Four looks at the current state of the collegiate function by examining curricula and enrollments and by exploring the attitudes of community college presidents. Chapter Five discusses the key arguments against a primary emphasis on the collegiate purpose. It also asks what accepting these arguments would mean to institutions and the national family of community colleges.

Chapter Six makes the case for the collegiate community college, describing the collegiate function, exploring its impact on comprehensiveness, and showing the gains that may be realized. Chapter Seven goes on to detail the actions that can be taken to strengthen the collegiate purpose at the institutional level, looking at curriculum, access, the associate degree, and general education. Going beyond the campus, it examines structural changes in the role of the community college, precollege education, and the relationship between two- and four-year schools. Chapter Eight places the discussion of collegiate purpose in the broader context of the nation's commitment to access to higher education.

This call to renew the collegiate purpose of the community college does not rely on descriptions of specific campus programs and services that focus on the collegiate function, followed by a request for replication of these efforts. Unfortunately, much of the literature describing specific institutional practices does not address the effectiveness of these efforts. In addition, few ongoing, careful analyses of current practices exist that might lead to policy formulation. Without first-hand confirmation of their effectiveness, their worth as collegiate undertakings remains unknown.

Instead, this book relies on generic descriptions of practices and programs that institutions can put in place. Throughout the book, many specific suggestions are given to help faculty, administrators, presidents, and trustees to strengthen the collegiate purpose of the community college. Before adopting any of these suggestions, however, community college faculty and administrators should carefully assess the likely success and effectiveness of those practices at their specific institutions.

The community college has done serious damage to itself

by becoming a site of compromised educational opportunity, a shadow of what it might be. Community colleges continue to offer access, but access to an experience that is intellectually "less than" the rest of higher education. By redefining educational opportunity in this way, the community colleges have systematically reduced the worth of access.

This book seeks to repair the damage, and to sustain a vision of the community college as a serious academic institution. It is a plea for the richest, most rewarding access that the community college can provide—access to the collegiate experience.

New York, New York   Judith S. Eaton
January 1994

The Author

Judith S. Eaton is president of the Council for Aid to Education in New York City. She received her B.A. degree (1964) from the University of Michigan in philosophy, her M.A. degree (1966), also from the University of Michigan, in history, and her Ph.D. degree (1975) from Wayne State University in education. She holds honorary degrees from Drexel University, Hahnemann University, and the Community College of Philadelphia.

Eaton has had an extensive career in community college education, serving as president of the Community College of Philadelphia and, earlier, the Community College of Southern Nevada. She has held various other administrative positions in the community college and has been a member of the teaching faculty in community colleges and four-year schools. Before joining the Council for Aid to Education, she was vice president of the American Council on Education. Eaton is the author of *The Unfinished Agenda: Higher Education and the 1980s* (1991) and editor of *Colleges of Choice: The Enabling Impact of the Community College* (1988) as well as the author of numerous articles and monographs.

Eaton has served on the board of directors of the American Association of Community Colleges and chaired the board in 1985. She has also been a member of the American Council on Education board of directors, which she chaired in 1988.

STRENGTHENING
COLLEGIATE
EDUCATION
in
COMMUNITY
COLLEGES

Chapter One

What It Means
to Be Collegiate

This book examines the collegiate community college — its origins, its present, and its future. It describes the collegiate community college, reviews its history, and explores its place within contemporary visions of the two-year institution. The book looks at arguments both in support of the collegiate community college and against it. It considers the capacity of institutions to sustain a collegiate function and the effect of the collegiate community college on the national commitment to access. It attempts to establish a conceptual foundation for the collegiate community college as well as to insist upon its importance, and it strongly argues that the future effectiveness of the community college requires a powerful collegiate commitment. Should the community college be a collegiate institution? Can it be? The response offered here is yes.

A *collegiate community college* is a community college with a *dominant collegiate function* or *strong collegiate commitment*. These three phrases will be used interchangeably throughout this discussion. As described here, a community college is considered collegiate when four conditions prevail. First, structured, sequential liberal arts and career education offerings dominate the curriculum, making up the majority of enrollments and offerings. Second, primary attention is given to developing students' college-level competencies through these offerings; these competencies are more important than, for example, precollege competencies earned in developmental and remedial programs.

Third, the community college environment, through the values faculty and administrators share with students, tries to ensure that students will be both interested in and prepared for baccalaureate study, whether it is pursued immediately after community college attendance or at some later point in a student's educational career. Fourth, the community college acknowledges its responsibility as a good citizen of the higher education community: it cooperates with other colleges and universities so that students, if they choose, will be able to transfer with ease.

College-level competence, a key commitment for the collegiate community college, requires a liberal arts or career education that routinely carries degree credit and is transferable. College-level study also requires the same degree of cognitive complexity as that of lower-division coursework at most colleges or universities in the country. Cognitive complexity that is adequate for college-level study emerges from intellectual norms that are easily recognizable and accepted within the higher education enterprise. These norms are embedded in the academic tasks that faculty require students to master. However, no more specific definitions of college-level work exist on which to anchor the notion of cognitive complexity.

A key test of college-level study is whether or not courses and programs are mobile — that is, transferable from one institution to another. This test includes not only the familiar two-year to four-year transfer, but also two-year to two-year and four-year to two-year transfer, examining the portability of the academic experience among a variety of higher education institutions. Another test of whether study is college-level is how the two-year institution itself categorizes it: if the study is designated as developmental or noncredit or not for degree credit or training, it is not college-level work. Another test is whether or not the four-year institution accepts this study in the form of its courses or programs. If a four-year school rejects lower-division coursework from a community college because it lacks sufficient cognitive complexity (rather than because the four-year institution may or may not offer the coursework), the work would not be considered college-level.

The definition of the collegiate function in this chapter varies from some earlier definitions in that it incorporates a commitment to applied fields (career education) as well as to the major disciplines of the liberal arts. This definition attempts to eliminate the artificial and unworkable distinction between academic and career areas of study by applying the college-level criterion to both. Academic education and career education are bound together by a shared commitment to college-level work.

The collegiate function as defined here places the community college firmly within higher education. Collegiate community colleges are neither extensions of high school nor one of the quasi-educational services offered by a community. The dominance of the collegiate function makes college-level studies the foundation of all institutional academic decision making. It is the core commitment that should set the agenda of the national leadership of the community college enterprise.

When the collegiate function is dominant within the community college, it defines and structures comprehensiveness. Comprehensiveness embodies the long-standing community college commitment to transfer, vocational, and community-based education and training. Collegiate community colleges can undertake some of the other programs and services that are identified with comprehensiveness provided that they are built upon a collegiate foundation. For example, although a dominant collegiate function does not preclude terminal vocational education that is not college-level, this type of education should not dominate the curriculum. The collegiate function also accepts the community-based function of the community college, but attention to community-based services should not be its dominant activity.

Many objections have been raised in the past to attempts to make the community college into a collegiate institution. These objections may be raised again in response to the arguments made here and will be considered in these pages. They center around the notion that a collegiate community college — as compared to other community colleges — somehow limits the scope of service of the two-year institution, diminishing responsiveness and comprehensiveness, contributing to educational elitism, and destroying educational opportunity. These objections have been effectively used to constrict the collegiate function of the community college in the past.

In addition to these objections, many long-standing features of community college life work against its collegiate success. Its tolerance of idiosyncratic student attendance patterns, the influence of narrowly focused vocational and demand-driven visions of the community college, the pressure of underprepared students, ongoing public misunderstanding of the educational role of the community college, and the prejudice of community college educators themselves against functioning as part of the higher education enterprise can — and do — coalesce to reduce the collegiate commitment of the community college. These features, coupled with the ongoing indifference of community college leaders, might even be sufficient, in the long run, to eliminate a collegiate interpretation of the community college's mission.

Should the Community College Be Collegiate?

Strong educational, social, and economic arguments exist for maintaining that the community college should be collegiate. To argue this point of view is to make a decision about what the community college ought to do — what is right for students and society. It is a public policy judgment that has strong social and moral overtones.

Educationally, the collegiate function is the community college's most powerful expression of the commitment to access, one that enhances the educational value of access in dramatic ways. Students in college-level liberal arts or career education programs receive the greatest actual and potential educational benefits of any group of students in the community college. There is a clear, documentable relationship between collegiate study and educational attainment.

Economically, the collegiate community college provides a greater return on investment for both students and taxpayers. Students in college-level courses and programs receive a more academically challenging education than those in other community college programs. This, in turn, provides them with greater mobility, enabling them to pursue the baccalaureate, a more demanding job, or both. It is the pathway to enhanced occupational status and increased earnings. Taxpayers, at present, invest less for a student in a community college than for a student in any other form of public higher education, and they have enjoyed a rich return on this investment: millions of students for whom higher education had not been economically feasible now attend college. This taxpayer investment does carry some risks, however. Although it is sound for some students, it has a negative side for others. Many underprepared students attend community colleges; the result, as some critics have pointed out, is that taxpayers are supporting students who are academically marginal and perhaps do not belong in college at all.

Socially, the community college is a pivotal educational institution for low-income students, individuals undergoing a major change in life circumstances, and especially minority students. The community college is on the front line of educational efforts to deal with racism, poverty, and undereducation. For the disadvantaged groups served by the community college, its collegiate experience is the richest educational opportunity they can have. It is central to assisting members of minority groups, who rely on the community college, to gain access to the baccalaureate, thereby correcting economic and social disparities based on race.

The collegiate community college is an extraordinary way for a democratic society to provide the best of higher education to as many people as can reasonably benefit. It is a profound statement of the unique value this country assigns to the individual and of its faith in the future. As a collegiate institution, the community college is unparalleled in providing, sustaining, and expanding educational opportunity and accomplishment within the society.

Can the Community College Be Collegiate?

As a result of its history and resources, and especially its faculty, the community college has a strong collegiate capacity. On the positive side, the collegiate community college has the benefit of continuity. An examination of the history of the educational role of the community college indicates that the collegiate function has consistently been a part of the two-year college. The liberal arts and transfer function was key to the establishment of the early junior college. Whether the collegiate function is measured by the commitment of the early junior college's leadership, its course and program offerings, or student enrollments, it is evident that a significant number of two-year colleges met the four conditions required to be collegiate institutions: a majority of enrollments and offerings were in structured, sequential liberal arts and career education; the offerings were at an appropriate level of cognitive complexity; the pursuit of longer-range educational goals constituted an important value in the institution, and students could transfer with ease.

The collegiate community college also has the benefit of significant internal resources. Financially, although support for community colleges on a full-time-equivalent basis is not as great as it should be, it does cover the actual cost of instruction in many college-level courses and programs. As far as staffing is concerned, many community college faculty have solid backgrounds in college-level study and retain a strong interest in the collegiate function. They are experienced, talented teachers who have met the most demanding challenges in American higher education. These teachers have taken on classrooms where student skills vary dramatically and have responded with creative approaches to teaching and curricula. Surveys consistently confirm their interest in the collegiate work of the community college. More than three-quarters of community colleges have a transfer function, and various community college curricula, both in liberal arts and career education, are, for the most part, considered college-level.

Externally, the development of a dominant collegiate function has been encouraged by the great national need for more challenging education, a better-informed citizenry, and a work force with flexible skills and an ability to think independently. The desire for social equality alone is a powerful incentive for a collegiate community college. Community colleges remain the single most important resource for economic and social gain through education. Establishment of a dominant collegiate function is a valuable response to public policy initiatives that address educational equity and the social justice needs of society.

The collegiate function has not been without challenge, however. Alternative visions of the community college that stress, for example, its role as a terminal-degree institution have limited the full expression of the collegiate role. The national leadership of the community college, over the years, has tended to ignore its collegiate role, and critics of the community college have strenuously questioned its collegiate capacity.

The collegiate role of the community college has also had serious competition over the years. Calling it a community college instead of a junior college had a particularly negative impact on the collegiate function: other community college purposes such as terminal occupational education, developmental and remedial education, and community services grew dramatically and the collegiate function diminished in scope and importance.

Although there is a significant historical foundation for the collegiate role, it has not enjoyed strong support from the official national leadership of the community college. Since 1959, in particular, that leadership has not given priority to the collegiate function; therefore, for more than thirty years, the collegiate function has received, at best, perfunctory support. As a result, when federal legislation, state legislation, and public policy focused on the community college, attention was concentrated on other purposes—especially on terminal occupational education.

Externally, many four-year educators and the general public do not believe that the community college is—or can be—a collegiate institution. They see it as being devoted solely to terminal vocational education, training, or developmental education and believe its only value to be that of providing skills for lower-wage, lower-status jobs. However well intentioned these individuals are, they contribute to a vision of the community college as a subcollegiate institution.

In spite of competition and limited leadership commitment,

the collegiate function has remained important in the community college. This is a tribute to both its vitality and the need that it meets. Given the survival of the collegiate function under these rather negative conditions, it is reasonable to be optimistic about establishing its dominance.

What a Collegiate Community College Will Mean

Several serious consequences are associated with advocacy of a dominant collegiate function in the community college. Some may view these consequences as a reason to firmly establish the collegiate function. Others may view them as an early warning about the difficulty of sustaining a dominant collegiate function. Still others will see the consequences as a serious obstacle to a dominant collegiate function and may choose to reject the collegiate emphasis as central to community college efforts.

1. *Creating a collegiate community college requires a choice between, historically, the three major visions of the contemporary community college.* Three compelling yet quite different perceptions of the community college's primary role have been proposed: (1) the community-based model as developed by Edmund Gleazer (president of the American Association of Community Colleges from 1959 to 1979), (2) the terminal occupational education model as developed by Dale Parnell (president of the American Association of Community Colleges from 1979 to 1991), and (3) the collegiate-comprehensiveness model as developed by Arthur Cohen and Florence Brawer (professors at the University of California, Los Angeles) (see Chapter Three). The Cohen-Brawer model is the only vision on which it makes sense to develop a collegiate community college.

2. *Building a collegiate community college redefines intellectual opportunity.* For students in the community college, the vision of intellectual opportunity cannot be confined to the community college experience. It must expand to incorporate the possibility that at some point in their lives, students may move on to other levels of education, especially the baccalaureate.

3. *A collegiate community college diminishes ambiguity about the community college's mission.* The educational role of the community

college has always been equivocal. A collegiate community college resolves this ambiguity. The community college is part of higher education. Its primary commitment is to college-level work. Its other programs and services are developed within its role as an institution of higher education that has a commitment to college-level work.

4. *A collegiate community college restricts the commitment to access.* This is not a choice between open and restricted access. The community college has always been a limited-access institution, but with fewer restrictions than other institutions that say they have open access or are nonselective. With a dominant collegiate function, the community college's commitment to access becomes even more restricted. Students must be prepared for college-level work and have, at most, modest remediation needs in order to enroll in most courses and programs. This is an expansion of the existing practice of limiting enrollments in some courses and programs based on demonstration of the skill levels needed for these undertakings. Students in need of serious remediation will have to attend other educational sites that can assist them in developing the skills needed for college-level work.

5. *A collegiate community college requires vigorous leadership to develop effective college-preparatory experiences outside the community college.* With a dominant collegiate function, the community college must diminish its responsibility for developmental and remedial education. Other educational sites such as transition schools (see Chapter 7) and, in the long run, improved elementary and secondary schools, must take primary responsibility for producing students who are ready for college. The community college alone cannot function as the complete answer to democratic education in the society. It takes the effective functioning of all levels of education to achieve this goal.

6. *A collegiate community college forces additional attention to be paid to its relationship to all other levels of education.* The community college is positioned squarely within higher education. This increases the need for coordination with four-year colleges and universities, especially in relation to transfer efforts. It also increases the community college's reliance on elementary and

secondary education because of the collegiate function's requirement that students be ready or nearly ready for college-level
work.

7. *A collegiate community college makes additional demands on
the nontraditional role of the community college.* Community colleges
will function as sites of nontraditional delivery of collegiate education in a nontraditional setting. The higher education
community—including the community college—has assumed
for too long that nontraditional students cannot avail themselves
of a collegiate education—that they cannot deal with the disciplines or the intellectual challenge of advanced work or enjoy
the benefits of scholarship. This assumption is false. Community colleges can take the lead in building models of collegiate
education provided in nontraditional ways.

8. *A collegiate community college accepts — and gains strength —
from some of the advice of its critics.* Stated in the most positive light,
critics of the community college have urged the community colleges to become serious academic institutions devoted to college-
level work: sequential, structured educational experiences that
will, at some point, help a large number of students to succeed
at the baccalaureate level. The critics seek this goal because they
believe that educational, economic, and social gains earned at
the baccalaureate level far exceed those earned at the associate-
degree level.

9. *A collegiate community college calls for reconsideration of the
associate degree.* The associate degree is a weak credential in the
community college. Even though its effect on students' educational gains is not clear, it is consistently used by many community colleges to structure the curriculum and make other important academic decisions. Structured, sequential educational
experiences *are* needed. If the associate degree is not an effective strategy to meet this need, others should be developed.

10. *A collegiate community college provides an extraordinary opportunity for faculty.* It can revitalize faculty commitment to teaching and learning and build an agenda for applied research and
scholarship. A dominant collegiate function can give community college faculty a national leadership role in shaping and
defining undergraduate education. It can help them to create

an intellectual community and to establish the community college as a serious academic institution.

Assumptions About the Collegiate Community College

The case for a collegiate community college presented here is based on several assumptions that need to be made explicit.

First, the argument for a dominant collegiate function does not claim that no community colleges are currently collegiate. Instead, it proceeds from an alternative premise: the extent to which community colleges are now collegiate needs to be expanded and strengthened. The collegiate function must be viewed as an urgent priority — an important goal driving community college decision making, agenda setting, and hopes for the future.

Second, the collegiate community college as envisioned here gives primary emphasis to levels of intellectual activity that have traditionally been limited to the nation's colleges and universities. It resists the expansion of collegiate study downward to include instruction characteristic of elementary and secondary education or outward to encompass the quasi-educational efforts of museums, civic organizations, and some corporations.

The third assumption is that the collegiate function can be reasonably carried out in a traditional campus-based environment. Strengthening the collegiate function does not require the community college to dramatically restructure itself using nontraditional delivery systems such as distance learning, interactive systems, or computer-based learning. Electronic technology is a highly desirable and dynamic resource that is exciting, beneficial, and useful in building a dominant collegiate function. The discussion here, however, explores the establishment of a dominant collegiate function in the context of a traditional academic environment that creatively uses these delivery systems.

Fourth, this book does not argue that a liberal arts, discipline-based education is the only suitable type of education for the community college. Although the words *college-level* suggest a liberal arts education, studies in these areas need not include only discipline-based modes of inquiry. General education is also a highly desirable means by which to strengthen the collegiate function.

Fifth, while the community college must retain its commitment to access and to assisting underprepared students, it makes a fundamental error when it honors this commitment by diluting its curricula and academic standards to something less than college-level work. The collegiate community college is academically demanding and there is a limit to the extent to which it can serve the underprepared. Community colleges can and should acknowledge this limit.

Sixth, this book does not assume that only academic work is collegiate and only occupational work is subcollegiate. Both can be either collegiate or subcollegiate, depending on their course content and level of intellectual challenge. The term *college-level career education* is used here to describe the occupationally influenced component of the collegiate function and *college-level liberal arts education* is used to describe the traditional disciplines, which are usually called academic studies. *Terminal* is applied to occupational or academic programs that are not collegiate.

Finally, the collegiate community college as described in these pages can and should be the focus of further serious research. This book can initiate an important and much-needed conversation about the community college as a collegiate institution. A research agenda can begin with an examination of the nation's community colleges to determine how many are collegiate institutions according to the criteria set down here. This should include attention to college-level study in order to more precisely define this important category. The research agenda should also devote significant time to documenting student learning gains in the collegiate community college. Research on these topics will provide a strong foundation for the future effectiveness of the community college as a collegiate institution.

Chapter Two

The Changing Roles of Two-Year Colleges

This chapter looks to the past. It examines the various educational roles the two-year college has played since its inception and asks how those roles contribute to building a collegiate community college. In doing so, it attempts to explode two myths. The first myth is that, in its earliest phase, the junior college functioned exclusively as a transfer or four-year college-preparatory institution. The second myth is that in a later phase, its transition from junior to community college unalterably committed it to terminal vocational education as its primary educational role.

Contrary to both myths, the two-year college has functioned as a multipurpose institution from its earliest days. Although the liberal arts and transfer function dominated the early two-year college, the occupational function was alive and well. Evidence from college catalogs, course enrollment figures, and the policy pronouncements of leaders of two-year colleges make this clear. Although the shift from junior to community college was accompanied by a significant increased emphasis on vocational education, this did not eclipse the earlier liberal arts and transfer function, but rather coexisted with it.

The two-year college, whether it is called a junior or community college, has always attempted to carry out a multipurpose educational role. Although there have been shifts in the emphasis on various curricula over the years, the ongoing commitment of community college educators to a multipurpose role is constant.

Some attention has always been given to college-level work, the liberal arts, the transfer function, and career education; this bodes well for the establishment of a dominant collegiate function.

Origins: The Early Junior College to 1940

Four major purposes are generally ascribed to the early junior college, the precursor to the community, junior, and technical colleges of the latter part of the twentieth century: a transfer and preparatory purpose, a preprofessional purpose, a terminal general education purpose, and a terminal occupational purpose.

The transfer and preparatory purpose was intended to provide a course of study in a two-year setting that was roughly equivalent in substance and standards to lower-division work at a four-year school. There was a presumption of shared curricular and pedagogical intent and activity between the two- and four-year institutions.

The preprofessional purpose provided preparation for occupationally focused baccalaureate education. It implicitly acknowledged that transfer preparation could extend beyond the disciplines and that universities housed an occupational function.

The general education purpose allowed students to undertake civic education. It was distinct from the transfer function in that it did not anticipate that students would necessarily move to four-year schools, and it differed from the occupational function in that it was not expected to lead to immediate employment and thus was not considered a vocational track.

Occupational was the generic term for curricula leading to employment. The term *vocational* had been used in early junior colleges to refer to studies in sales, trade, or agriculture. *Semiprofessional* referred to manufacturing, business, and service occupations as well as to positions as engineering technicians, general assistants, and laboratory technicians. *Technical* referred to the scientific and industrial fields. After the 1950s, *career education* was used synonymously with the generic term *occupational* (Cohen and Brawer, 1989).

Three educational issues drove the development of the early junior college: the debate over the scope, nature, and definition of secondary education; the role and purpose of the associate degree; and efforts at the university level to separate specialized learning from general education (Diener, 1986). All of these issues emerged from discussions about whether or not the university should be engaged in lower-division education. The concept of the two-year college was attractive to those who wished to minimize the university's responsibility at this level of education. Other factors affecting the emergence of the two-year college were efforts to imitate European systems of education, university presidents who sought to establish their institutions as centers of advanced study without the distraction of offering lower-division undergraduate work, the extension of universities into communities, the role of private enterprise in transferring older academies into junior colleges and in establishing new institutions, the impact of public education, and the belief that some four-year institutions would make better junior colleges (Bogue, 1950).

These factors and issues produced four types of two-year institutions between 1900 and 1920: the junior college or lower division of a college of liberal arts or a university, normal schools accredited for two years of college work, public high schools that had been extended to include the first two years of college work, and small private colleges that limited their college work to two years (McDowell, 1919).

The primary sources of information about the purposes of the early junior college are the writings of its key leaders, data on student enrollment, and information on curricular offerings. Together, they provide a profile of the early junior college's educational role.

The Writings of Key Leaders

Several streams of thought converged in the early years of the development of the junior college. They included the thinking of university presidents and educators such as Henry P. Tappan at The University of Michigan, William Rainey Harper at the University of Chicago, and Alexis F. Lange at the University of California. Others such as Leonard V. Koos, W. C. Eells, and Doak S. Campbell provided leadership for the emergence of the community college as a national enterprise. These national spokespersons focused on the educational role of the junior college as it related to contemporary visions of the university. They were also concerned with what came to be called the mission of the junior college — the guiding self-image of this emerging institution.

McDowell (1919) contends that "the university must be held responsible for the first suggestion of the junior college idea in the United States" (p. 16). University leaders sought a new educational vehicle for lower-division undergraduate work. They maintained that the first and second years of college were more appropriate as secondary education, and that students entering the university should be prepared for specialized work (Bogue, 1950). Harper recommends separating first- and second-year students from those at the junior level or higher. This would involve changes both in high schools and in some four-year colleges. Harper, along with U.S. Commissioner P. P. Claxton, urges struggling four-year institutions to become two-year schools that focus on lower-division work; he sees a need for high schools to take responsibility for this work as well. Harper sees five advantages to the junior college. First, it provides the convenience of ending college work after the sophomore year. Second, it offers an opportunity to expand the educated population to those who might not pursue university work. Third, it would allow standards to be increased in professional schools. Fourth, it would encourage expanded offerings in academies and high schools. And finally, it would provide better use of the resources of struggling four-year colleges (Harper in Diener, 1986).

Tappan (in Diener, 1986) argues for a major distinction between college and university work. His concept of the university is based upon the German model of research and advanced study, which requires universities to provide libraries, materials for learning, professors, and research capacity. To sustain this model, other educational institutions, including two-year colleges, need to carry out the responsibilities of lower-division work. Tappan describes a college as an elementary and preparatory school that may or may not be attached to a university. University work presumes that college work has been completed.

Lange (1918) describes the junior college in a manner that is strikingly similar to that of Dale Parnell's description many years later. The junior college is a vehicle for "training for vocations occupying the middle ground between those of the artisan type and the professions" (p. 213). Lange sees this as a "middle vocational system" that produces the scientific farmer, the trained city employee, and the highly skilled mechanic. According to him, junior colleges need to provide an alternative to university-type training (Brint and Karabel, 1989). Vocational education is central for Lange; he says, "I am more than skeptical about the educational success of any junior college with only nonvocational departments" (p. 214). Although he supports departments of civic education that are partly vocational and maintains that foundation courses developed in cooperation with the university are needed, Lange places the junior college within a secondary education system that is also composed of the junior high school and high school. For Lange, "the junior college is the apex, the point of fulfillment of public school education. It provides a liberal education for those who cannot attend a college or a university, a vocational training for others" (Diener, 1986, p. 67).

Those who struggled with the early identity of the junior college had two major concerns: (1) ensuring that purposes other than transfer and preparatory ones could be strengthened and (2) establishing an appropriate educational place for the junior college, whether in secondary or higher education. They emerged with a vision of an institution with a range of purposes that went beyond an initial interest in preparatory work for the university to an expanded commitment to general, occupational, and civic education. This set the stage for the major commitment to occupational education and community-based education that the community colleges made in the 1960s and 1970s. As early as the 1920 meeting in Saint Louis that spearheaded the establishment of the American Association of Junior Colleges (AAJC), it was clear that there were important differences of opinion about the identity or mission of the junior college. As with contemporary discussions of the two-year college, the only agreement was that the junior college should be a multipurpose institution. This was followed by disagreement about the number of purposes it should have and the extensiveness of any single purpose.

The early leaders of the junior college also differed among themselves about the place of this institution in the educational enterprise. Koos saw junior colleges as part of secondary education. Eells envisioned them as part of higher education. Seashore viewed them as transitional institutions. Bogue considered them to be autonomous institutions that were not positioned within existing educational niches (Cohen and Associates, 1971). There was even some discussion about the possibility of establishing four-year junior colleges that awarded the baccalaureate (Brick, 1964). The issue of the place of the junior college within the educational structure of the country had an impact on efforts to determine what programs the junior college should emphasize and what its educational role should be.

The discussion about a proper program emphasis for the junior college continued throughout the 1930s. While there was general agreement that the transfer and preparatory function was effective, concerns were consistently expressed about the limited development of its other purposes (Barton, 1935; Campbell, 1932–1933). Brint and Karabel (1989) maintain that the majority of junior college presidents thought that their institutions should be primarily terminal, while approximately 30 percent believed that the transfer function was the most important. Brint and Karabel state: "The dominant sensibility among junior college administrators who favored terminal programs combined meritocratic assumptions with social engineering goals. Most junior college students, these administrators argued, were not suitable candidates for professional training in the universities and should therefore be trained for the best jobs available to them" (p. 56).

Eells, perhaps the most far-ranging and influential commentator on the early junior college, places the junior college within higher education, but sees it as a complex and diverse institution that goes beyond some of the standard activities of collegiate schools. He sets the stage for the excitement — and the difficulty — of the attempt by the comprehensive community college to do so much for so many people. His classic 1931 study (Eells, 1931a) calls attention to this expansion of purpose as it was reflected in the changing AAJC definition of the junior college between 1922 and 1929. Eells says that in 1922, the AAJC maintained that "the junior college is an institution offering two years of instruction of strictly collegiate grade" (p. 3). By 1929, the association had adopted a new definition that was much longer and more complex:

> The junior college, as at present constituted, comprises several different forms of organization: first, a two-year institution embracing two years of collegiate work in advance of the completion of what is ordinarily termed the twelfth grade of an accredited secondary school; secondly, the institution embracing two years of standard collegiate work integrated with one more contiguous year of fully accredited high school work administered as a single unit. The aims of the curriculum in either case are to meet the needs of the student for maximum growth and development, to further his social maturity, and to enable him to make his greatest contribution as a member of society [Eells, 1931a, pp. 167–168].

In this context, Eells identifies four functions for the junior college. The *popularizing* function is the junior college's access responsibility: high school graduates or adults can obtain education of a general nature. The *preparatory* function provides the education required for students to transfer to a university. The *terminal* function provides vocational courses for specific occupations and immediate employment. The *guidance* function pays attention to the personal welfare of students, improving their thinking capacity and ensuring that each student gains from the college experience (Thomas, 1927). Junior colleges should provide general education, the site for the needed thirteenth and fourteenth grades, a way to protect the role and status of the university to do upper-division and graduate studies, and a place for university preparatory work.

Koos (1925), carefully reviewing the first two decades of the junior college through surveys, articles, addresses, and early college catalogs, affirms the complex role of the junior college. He also tries to identify its special purpose. While acknowledging that providing work acceptable to universities is the most widely recognized purpose of the junior college, he also maintains that it is the least distinctive. The purposes he considers special to the junior college are providing terminal general education, supplying quality instruction, increasing the attention paid to individual students, developing leadership, connecting the home and school for immature students, and reorganizing secondary and higher education. In addition to conceptualizing the junior college as a multipurpose institution, Koos also urges a restructuring of education to the 6-4-4 plan, which would more closely identify junior college with elementary and secondary education rather than with higher education. This plan provides for six years of elementary school, four years of junior high school, and four years of high school and junior college. Although Koos's vision of the educational role of the junior college was highly influential, his restructuring proposal was not.

Campbell (1930) restates the purposes of the junior college, based on his study of 404 institutions in 1929. In doing so, he reaffirms the multipurpose character of these institutions. According to Campbell, the junior college should be identified with secondary school and should constitute the final two years of a four-year program. Junior colleges should be both geographically and financially accessible for those who could not otherwise attend college and should provide vocational education "above the trades but below the professional and technological schools of university grade" (p. 83). Finally, junior colleges should avoid duplication and overlapping of courses that are available at other educational levels.

Campbell (1932-1933) goes beyond a restatement of purpose to ask for a description of the distinctive contribution of the junior college, warning that if this institution has a particular philosophy, it should be stated, and that the educational aim of the junior college should be determined. Campbell points out that the junior college curriculum does not differ greatly from the lower-division university curriculum, and he questions the longer-range appropriateness of this fact, but without offering suggestions for curricular change or expansion. Others agree. Barton (1935), for example, stresses the junior college's historic indebtedness to the university. He points out that the perceived need to adhere to admissions and other standards of accreditation associations (heavily influenced by the universities) has kept the transfer and preparatory purpose central and limited the curricular expansion needed to meet the other stated purposes.

Weersing (1931) reflects a similar concern. He points out that, as the junior college moved into its third decade, its aims and purposes, as well as the "philosophy peculiar to it," were not clear. Weersing identifies four misconceptions about the junior college: first, that the institution ought to have "full collegiate status"; second, that junior college courses should be "equivalent" to university courses; third, that the junior college should be primarily a vocational school; and fourth, that the junior college needs to segregate transfer and occupational education. Weersing maintains that a desire to change the educational system undergirded the establishment of the junior college and that it was not created only to sustain existing higher education practices. Some of these institutions of higher education were not meeting emerging social needs. Weersing supports the junior college as an institution committed to an integrated program of liberal arts, general education, and occupational education. He is opposed to viewing it as a place primarily dedicated to vocational training, and he discourages curricular configurations that segregate liberal arts and occupational education.

The Junior College Legacy

The university presidents and educators who were central to the early establishment of the junior college were particularly motivated by their interest in their institutions' ability to provide advanced study without the distraction of lower-division work. They believed that they could pursue this goal while, at the same time, strengthening education in several ways. The junior college would enhance access by making more education available locally and at low cost, expand the scope of studies after high school, and, in general, reach an audience of potential students hitherto unserved by existing universities.

The early leaders of the junior college enterprise struggled to identify the kinds of education to which the junior college should be devoted as well as to resolve the issue of the place of the junior college — whether it should be considered secondary or higher education. Their writings, at least in the early years, consistently supported the notion of the junior college as a multipurpose institution involving transfer and preparatory, preprofessional, general, and occupational education. They were articulating a vision of this new educational unit and, in doing so, they attempted to address the relationships between the various purposes. They were confronted with questions such as how much occupational education should be offered and what should be the role of general education in the curriculum.

In particular, Eells's consistent championing of the need for expanded occupational education led some observers to see him as spearheading the strong emphasis on occupational education in the junior college. According to Frye, "Eells was the chief spokesman for the view that the principal function of the junior college was terminal education. Before 1940, there were few voices of opposition to this dominant view" (Frye, 1992, p. 53). Eells led the junior college leadership and, by 1940, there was agreement that two-thirds to three-quarters of junior college students should be enrolled in terminal vocational programs (Brint and Karabel, 1989). This interpretation, however, did not give equal weight to his firm support for the other purposes of the junior college.

In many ways, these national spokespersons began a dialogue about the role, purpose, and place of the junior college that is still under way. In general, they acknowledged the strength of transfer education over general or occupational education and were divided on whether to locate the junior college at the top of secondary education or at the bottom of higher education. Maintaining that university education was not appropriate for most junior college students, they urged further emphasis on terminal education, envisioning the primary purpose of the junior college as the education of students for the middle group of occupations, between artisan and professional. It is not clear whether the writings of Koos, Eells, and Campbell were at the heart of a major vocationalizing effort in the junior college and were central to establishing an "ideology of vocationalism" (Brint and Karabel, 1989). What is clear is that they were committed to strengthening terminal and occupational studies *in addition to* transfer and preparatory education in order to serve students for whom university education was not an option. It is easy to acknowledge the support of Koos, Eells, and Campbell for occupational education without going so far as to acknowledge as correct Brint and Karabel's contention that this constituted advocacy of education for acquiescence — "educated fellowship" — as distinct from education for independence or critical thinking.

Curricula and Enrollment of the Early Junior College

However powerful and provocative were the statements of leaders in the growing junior college enterprise, the curricula of these institutions speak in an even louder voice. It is the curriculum that truly defines an institution, describes its values, and answers fundamental questions about its aims and purpose. In the early junior college, curricula were first and foremost devoted to the preparatory function for future liberal arts or professional study. Terminal education for occupational or general purposes received rhetorical attention considerably in excess of actual offerings or enrollments.

Listening to the voice of the curriculum also requires a distinction to be made between what a junior college offers and what students choose to study. The enrollment of junior college students in various programs is sometimes confused with institutional statements of curricular offerings. Enrollments are the voice of the students. The courses and programs described in catalogs indicate, among other things, institutional intent, but statements of available curricula do not tell us to what extent students avail themselves of these offerings.

Curricular Offerings. The early curricular offerings of the junior college were primarily in traditional liberal arts areas, although terminal and occupational offerings increased in the early twentieth century. Studies of early junior college curricula (Barton, 1935; Campbell, 1930; Colvert, 1947; Koos, 1925) acknowledge that the earliest junior college had, as Barton puts it, "its course of study given to it" (p. 405) — that is, the standard fare of the first and second year offered by a four-year college or university. McDowell (1919), too, maintains that the preparatory aims of the junior college came first, followed by cultural-terminal or "rounding out" education. Koos (1925) documents that 95 percent of public junior colleges and 90 percent of private junior colleges had courses designed for the preparatory purpose. Twenty percent of public and 12 percent of private junior colleges had courses designed for rounding out education. Fifty-three percent of public junior colleges and 48 percent of private junior colleges had coursework designed for the semiprofessional purpose. McDowell (1919) surveys twenty-eight private and nineteen public junior colleges for 1917–18 and finds that "traditional freshman and sophomore college subjects" were most likely to be offered. There was a difference between public and private junior colleges: public junior colleges were more likely to house vocational offerings than private institutions. Eighteen percent of offerings in public colleges and 9 percent of offerings in private colleges are classified by McDowell as vocational.

Koos (1925) maintains that, of the various purposes of the junior college he identifies, the area of greatest agreement is that of four-year preparatory work. His data show that only 22 percent of the curricular offerings of twenty-three public and thirty-five private junior colleges during 1921–22 were in agriculture, commerce, education, engineering and industry, home economics, and other occupational areas. Eells (1931a), reviewing seven curricular studies undertaken during the 1920s, confirms that liberal arts offerings were dominant in public and private junior colleges.

Campbell (1930) reports that, of 343 junior colleges, 147 gave preparatory education as a stated purpose in the catalog; 73, occupational education; 71, moral and religious training; 48, "completion education"; 18, adult education; and 7, exploration and orientation. He goes on to compare stated purposes with actual offerings and finds that 312 institutions gave preparatory offerings as a stated purpose; 216, vocational offerings; 111, preprofessional offerings; and 75, terminal offerings. Campbell concludes from this that the terminal function was more prominent in the literature than in actual offerings. Barton (1935) concurs, pointing out that courses dealing with terminal education did not keep pace with the expressed aims for terminal education.

Colvert (1947) documents that, over time, terminal course offerings increased as a percentage of total offerings. According to McDowell (1919), terminal courses made up 17.5 percent of total semester-hour offerings in 1917. Koos, in 1921, reports 28 percent of total semester-hour offerings to be in terminal courses. Eells, in 1930, indicates that in that year, 33 percent of semester-hour offerings were in terminal courses. Colvert states that this had dropped to 32 percent by 1947. He offers two explanations for this. First, junior colleges, as new institutions, sought sanction for their efforts through, for example, accreditation. By providing traditional offerings such as the first two years of university coursework, they became familiar to accreditation agencies and thus more likely to receive the recognition they sought. Second, it could cost more to offer occupational education in cases where specialized equipment or facilities were required. Eells (1941) confirms this significant increase in vocational offerings in junior colleges from 1917 to 1935. He estimates that one-third of all offerings in junior colleges around the country were in nonacademic or terminal fields.

Enrollment. Enrollment data for the early junior college are limited. Those that are available document the general growth of enrollments, the growth of terminal and occupational enrollments, and the continued dominance of the transfer and preparatory purpose. Gleazer (1959), looking at general enrollments (student head count) in junior colleges between 1900 and 1958, identifies 8 junior colleges enrolling 100 students in 1900–01 and 610 institutions enrolling 236,152 students in 1939–40. During this period of significant growth in enrollment, the number of public junior colleges outstripped the number of private institutions, housing 71 percent of enrollments in 1938–39. Although the first 8 junior colleges were private institutions, by 1938–39, 55 percent of the 575 junior colleges were private, with 258 public institutions in existence.

Prior to 1938–39, no national data on enrollments in junior college terminal programs were collected (Eells, 1941). In 1938–39, 34 percent of the students in 426 junior colleges were classified as being enrolled in terminal curricula. An earlier study in 1931 examined 61 publicly controlled junior colleges and identified 20 percent of the students as being enrolled in terminal courses.

Hillmer (1949), looking at occupational enrollments, compares terminal curricula in 1947–48, 1938–39, and 1930–31. He reports that data from 104 public junior colleges show 47 percent of their student bodies enrolled in terminal programs. Christensen had reported terminal-program enrollments as 20 percent of total enrollments in 1930–31 and Eells reported terminal-program enrollments as 35 percent of total enrollments in 1938–39. Taylor (1933) indicates that in 1933, 80 percent of enrollments in 153 junior colleges around the country were in college-preparatory curricula. Taylor warned his colleagues that the junior college had not yet come to grips with the aims of its curricula, calling this perhaps the most serious problem in American higher education. This lack of direction gave rise to adverse criticism.

Analysis of curricular offerings and student enrollments shows that the early junior college was, for the most part, a traditional academic institution offering primarily liberal arts courses that would be used for transfer to a four-year institution. As Frye (1992) points out, advocacy for occupational education had limited impact on junior colleges. However committed to occupational education junior college leaders were, the views they articulated had little effect on curricula and enrollment, the spread of junior colleges, or the attitudes of the local communities in which they were founded. The transfer function was obvious and dominant, and its relative popularity compared to that of terminal education did not wane.

In the face of the dominance of the transfer and preparatory purpose, the emphasis by the key leadership on the junior college as a multipurpose institution may be explained by their desire to ensure that the other purposes of the junior college should become as viable as the transfer and preparatory purpose. Arguments to "vocationalize" the junior college (Brint and Karabel, 1989; Frye, 1992) are based on the interpretation that the leadership emphasized only the terminal occupational function and did so at the particular expense of the transfer and preparatory purpose. However, the writings of the national spokespersons do not reflect this singlemindedness of intent.

The Transition to Community Colleges, 1940–1970

The 1940s saw the end of World War II, the initiation of the Servicemen's Readjustment Act, and the Truman Commission—all of which had a dramatic impact on junior colleges. In the 1950s and 1960s, four major legislative events—the National Defense Education Act of 1958, the Vocational Education Act of 1963, the Civil Rights Act of 1964, and the Higher Education Act of 1965—helped to produce, by 1970, a two-year college that differed significantly from the junior college of the early twentieth century. It differed in emphasis, size, the nature of its programming, and the composition of its student body.

Many observers of the two-year college see the post–World War II period as pivotal in its transition from junior college to community college status. Thornton (1960), Monroe (1972), and Hillway (1958) discuss a shift or a repositioning of two-year colleges in which *community* rather than *junior* became the dominant descriptor. Bogue (1950) maintains that *community college* better describes the two-year college. *Junior* describes, in his view, a restricted function and is neither accurate nor inclusive in relation to the community needs that these institutions must meet. To be a community college, an institution has to serve the community, subject itself to local control or control determined by the citizens of the community, and receive financial support that includes state aid, local tax revenues, and equalization funds for poorer communities.

The socioeconomic conditions of the country following the war, the growing demand for occupational education, an increased interest in adult education, and, increasingly, community needs were driving factors in the educational policy decisions made by two-year institutions. For some, moving from junior to community college status helped to clarify institutional identity and direction. Monroe (1972) contends that "until the 1950s, community college leaders seemed confused as to what type of institution a community college really was" (p. 22). Thornton (1960) sees acceptance of responsibility for service to adults in the community as the pivotal factor in this transition. Hillway (1958) regards the period after 1945 as the "real" starting point of the community college, "for it was about this time that the community-serving function of the two-year college was widely recognized and accepted" (p. 42).

George Zook (1940), president of the American Council on Education (ACE), addressing the twentieth-anniversary meeting of the AAJC, looked both to the past and to the future of junior colleges. For the past, he contended that junior colleges had established the acceptance of certain educational concepts in the country. These are the concepts of lower-division general education, occupational terminal education, education for commuter students, and undergraduate education that frees the university to pursue advanced study. These purposes, curricula, and enrollments characterized much of the functioning of the two-year college until 1940. For the future, Zook urged his colleagues to stress these concepts as well as the concept of cooperative education. He also recommended that all states establish a system of junior colleges that would be cultural leaders in their local communities.

The Servicemen's Readjustment Act and the Truman Commission

The Servicemen's Readjustment Act, or GI Bill, of 1944 provided the financial means for veterans to attend an institution of higher education. The Act reflected the obligation of the nation to its service personnel and a desire to return them to the work force. It also helped to initiate a radical enrollment growth in higher education. In 1944–45, two-year enrollments stood at 295,475; seven years later, in 1951–52, enrollments had doubled to 562,786; and ten years later, in 1954–55, they had reached 696,321 (Gleazer, 1959). Between 1939–40 and 1949–50, four-year enrollments grew from 1,238,500 to 2,177,700 (Ottinger, 1984). The Servicemen's Readjustment Act also initiated a major change in public policy toward the collegiate experience in American life. Higher education was not to be confined to the few, but was to be available to a much broader spectrum of citizens.

The President's Commission on Higher Education was established by Harry Truman in 1947 and chaired by George Zook. It was charged with "the task of defining the responsibilities of colleges and universities in American democracy and in international affairs—and more specifically, with reexamining the objectives, methods, and facilities of higher education in the United States in the light of the social role it has to play" (*Higher Education for American Democracy*, 1947, p. 1). The Commission advocated major expansion of higher education, and community colleges were central to this effort. The Commission maintained that these institutions should increase in number and further diversify their activities. It lent its support to the two-year college as a community college rather than a junior college; it then identified "educational service to the entire community" as the purpose of the community college. This meant that the community college should provide educational opportunity and meet community needs for both young people and adults. Although it should emphasize terminal education that is both general and occupational, it should not abandon its commitment to collegiate studies. The community college should be a center for learning in the community.

The Truman Commission was a watershed in the history of the two-year college. With the Truman Commission Report, the community role of the community college gained ascendancy over its academic role. The college conceived as a site of intellectual development of the individual gave way to the college seen as the site of a range of educational experiences that would benefit the community. Even though other higher education institutions might place their responsibility to intellectual development first and only then consider the implications for community development, the Truman Commission charged the community college to place its community responsibility first and its role in intellectual development second. This was done in spite of the report's commitment to the collegiate and general education functions of the community college.

The effect of the Truman Commission's work was to consolidate earlier efforts by the junior college to create a unique identity for the two-year institution. Again, the liberal arts and transfer function did not ensure a unique place for two-year schools. The Truman Commission, by marrying educational opportunity and community need to the junior college's efforts to emphasize occupational education, had the effect of encouraging community colleges to move away from the mainstream of higher education. It also had the effect of undermining the collegiate function.

The Truman Commission Report has assumed almost mythic importance in the eyes of community college leaders because it affirmed three principles: equal opportunity in higher education, higher education for all the population and not just a special elite, and the principle of the two-year college as, in the words of James Thornton (1960), a "community-serving junior college" — an institution devoted to offering the kinds of programming that meet demonstrated community need. The Truman Commission launched the contemporary community college and its accompanying commitment to access. It had the effect of increasing the community college's prominence and assisting it in its quest for legitimacy. The Commission's central goal of extending educational opportunity required a greatly expanded community college enterprise. According to Brint and Karabel (1989), "For a movement wracked by feelings of insecurity and marginality from its beginning, the public recognition that it had sought for so long finally arrived" (p. 71).

Federal Legislation and the Community College

Through the National Defense Education Act (NDEA), the Civil Rights Act, the Vocational Education Act (VEA), and the Higher Education Act (HEA), the federal government had a major impact on the educational role of the community college. Three explicit commitments were particularly important: the commitment to ensure that federal grant and loan programs provided the financial foundation to make the public policy commitment to equal opportunity genuine, the commitment to include members of racial minorities in the access efforts of community colleges, and the commitment to provide special funding for programs that would lead to immediate employment.

The NDEA and HEA were pivotal in the rapidly expanding enrollments of the community college after 1965. This legislation provided for a national program of grants and loans to students wishing to attend institutions of higher education. Between 1969 and 1979, federal support to community colleges went from 6 percent to 8.4 percent (Brint and Karabel, 1989). In 1975–76, two-year institutions were allocated $420 million, or 8 percent of the federal dollars available to higher education, and by 1984–85, this had increased to $1.4 billion, or 10 percent. Grants to two-year institutions were 7 percent in 1975–76 and 11 percent in 1984–85 (El-Khawas, Carter, and Ottinger, 1988).

The VEA was a direct stimulant to the expansion of terminal vocational programs in the community college. The act made federal dollars available to support vocational education schools; vocational work-study programs; and research, training, and demonstrations in vocational education. The VEA and its amendments of 1968 broadened criteria for federal assistance to courses that did not lead to the baccalaureate. Congress provided $42.9 million in 1968, $707 million in 1972, and $981 million in 1974 (Lombardi, 1978, citing Davenport and others, 1976). In 1984, the VEA was supplanted by the Carl D. Perkins Vocational Education Act, which provided aid to states to make vocational programs accessible to the handicapped, the disadvantaged, single parents, homemakers, and the incarcerated (National Center for Education Statistics, 1991). By 1985, community colleges received more than $16 million in vocational funds. At the same time, vocational enrollments grew and the number of vocational programs increased in New York, Illinois, Florida, and Hawaii (Cohen and Brawer, 1989).

The Civil Rights Act and especially Executive Order 11246 (dealing with affirmative action), combined with the changing demographics of the school-age population, resulted in a significant expansion of minority enrollments in community colleges. Minority enrollments grew from 759,800 (out of 3,879,100 total students) in 1976 to 1,106,900 (out of 4,868,100) in 1988 (National Center for Education Statistics, 1991). This outstripped minority enrollment growth in the four-year sector.

What Emerged: Community Colleges from 1970 to 1990

The early junior college mission—an amalgam of transfer, general education, and occupational education as described by the pioneer national spokespersons—was modified during the twenty-five-year period after World War II through increased emphasis on occupational and community-based education. In addition, by 1970, the community college's mission statement had expanded beyond a primary commitment to the four junior college purposes to include noncredit vocational training, community service programs of a quasi-educational nature, and social services such as child care. Brint and Karabel (1989) describe this as the result of "the tendency of junior college administrators to withdraw from the academic hierarchy of higher education institutions and occupy the apex of an alternative nonacademic hierarchy" (p. 79). Frye (1992) points out that the uncertainty of purpose that accompanied the early junior college still exists in the contemporary community college. He cites Jennings Wagoner, who, in 1985, described the community college as "uncertain of its identity, unsure of its place in the post-secondary community, and unable to determine its institutional priorities" (p. 3). Community colleges also experienced a dramatic increase in the number and size of institutions. They were bigger and more complex, served a more heterogeneous student population, and had developed flexible academic standards using strategies such as nonpunitive grading, formative approaches to assessment, and individualized instruction.

Size

During the 1960s, community college enrollment quadrupled, reaching 2.3 million, while at the same time total university enrollment doubled (Karabel, 1974). Karabel reports that between 1970 and 1982 the number of students increased by 215 percent, from 2,223,000 to 4,772,000 (Zwerling, 1986). By 1989, enrollments stood at 5,083,461 (National Center for Education Statistics, 1991). In 1945–46, there were 648 two-year colleges. The number of institutions peaked at 1,230 in 1975–76 (American Association of Community and Junior Colleges, 1991). In addition to growth in aggregate numbers of community colleges and in the number of community college students, the large enrollment increases also produced great variation in size among two-year institutions. In 1990, for example, the nation's largest community college enrolled 113,380 students (American Association of Community and Junior Colleges, 1991); in the same year, smaller community colleges enrolled as few as 1,000 students. As of 1991, the American Association of Community Colleges reported that approximately 25 percent of community colleges enrolled more than 6,000 students, 50 percent enrolled 1,600 to 6,000 students, and 25 percent enrolled fewer than 1,600 students. Changes in size produced more institutions and more varied institutions.

Programming

Changes in programming in the community college were marked by three characteristics: a significant increase in occupational education, diminution of the transfer function, and a major expansion of noncredit, community-based offerings. Occupational education expanded in two ways. More degree programs were offered in occupational education—and more courses were taken for credit by students—and more noncredit training programs were offered. Community service offerings—especially noncredit personal interest courses—became a staple of community college programming. Developmental and remedial, or precollege-level, studies became increasingly frequent.

By 1940, terminal or vocational programs were offered in 70 percent of two-year colleges compared with 14 percent in 1917 and 29 percent in 1921 (Cohen and Brawer, 1989). Since the 1960s, career education enrollments have grown faster than liberal arts enrollments. In 1963, career enrollments (219,766) made up 26 percent of total enrollments (847,572). By 1975, they made up 35 percent, with 1,389,516 students out of 4,001,970 enrolled in career education (Cohen and Brawer, 1989). The American Association of Community and Junior Colleges (1986) estimates even greater occupational enrollment growth: occupational enrollments increased from 13 percent in 1965 to 50 percent in 1976. State reports from the mid 1960s indicate that occupational enrollments grew along with total enrollments and outstripped transfer enrollments (Lombardi, 1978). By 1975–76, more than 55 percent of associate degrees were awarded in occupational areas, and by 1979–80, other associate degrees were at their lowest percentage (37.5 percent) since 1970 (Brint and Karabel, 1989). In the 1970s and early 1980s, growth was greatest in conventional, "low-tech" fields such as nursing, dental hygiene, automotive and construction trades, police, firefighting, child care, business, and commerce. Data processing, electronics, and health care technologies grew at a slower rate. Since 1979, however, these high-tech programs have dominated the growth of the community college (Grubb, 1984).

The liberal arts and transfer purpose has contracted over the years. Enrollments in the liberal arts, although remaining the mainstay of the junior and community college, diminished and then remained stable. Liberal arts study, which made up 75 percent of the curriculum in the junior college, has stabilized at just over 50 percent since the 1970s (Cohen and Brawer, 1987). The transfer function has also declined over the years.

Transfer education made up 60 to 70 percent of enrollments until the late 1960s (Lombardi, 1979). Since the 1970s, transfer estimates, to the extent that they are available, range from 20 to 30 percent (Palmer and Eaton, 1991). In addition, the cognitive complexity of liberal arts and transfer work has been diminished by asking students to do less work and less demanding work. They are assigned less writing, for example, and the level of demand of reading and writing assignments has decreased (Cohen and Brawer, 1987; Richardson, Fisk, and Okun, 1983).

Community service, or predominantly noncredit programming in occupational or personal interest areas, was virtually unknown in the early part of the century. By 1975–76, more than four million students were registered in continuing education and noncredit adult programs (Lombardi, 1978). By 1988, this programming embraced a noncredit enrollment of 6,117,757 (Mahoney, 1990). Data concerning the extent of developmental and remedial education in the early junior college are not available. For the contemporary community college, in the 1980s, developmental and remedial education enrollments increased (Cohen and Brawer, 1989). In 1990–91, 98.8 percent of public two-year institutions offered remedial instruction or tutoring (National Center for Education Statistics, 1991).

Students

The most obvious change in the student body has been demographic. Community colleges went from serving a predominantly white male population to a predominantly female population that included more members of racial minorities. In 1970, two-year institutions enrolled 2,319,385 students; data on minority students are not available for that year. In 1976, they enrolled 3,883,321 students, of whom 759,000 were minorities (National Center for Education Statistics, 1991). In 1990, two-year colleges enrolled 5,181,000 students, of whom 1,189,000 were minorities. This is a shift from 19.5 percent to 22.9 percent. This small percentage of increase at the national level masks the dramatic demographic change that has affected individual institutions, shifting them from overwhelmingly white to predominantly minority enrollments.

In Fall 1970, women made up 43 percent of college enrollments. In 1989, their numbers had grown to 57 percent (National Center for Education Statistics, 1991). Part-time enrollment grew from 1,090,474 out of a total enrollment of 2,319,385, or 47 percent, in 1970 to 3,251,689 out of a total enrollment of 5,083,461, or 63.9 percent, in 1989 (National Center For Education Statistics, 1991). In 1982, 21 percent of students from the highest socioeconomic quartile enrolled in community colleges, while 58 percent enrolled in senior institutions. In that same year, 16 percent of students from the highest academic quartile enrolled in community colleges; 63 percent enrolled in senior institutions (Cohen, 1988). Before World War II, community colleges were predominantly middle-class institutions. After the war, they became predominantly lower-middle-class and working-class institutions (Brint and Karabel, 1989).

Cross, describing community college students in 1968, maintains that these students had lower educational and occupational aspirations than those in four-year schools. They were uncertain about their future and many did not pursue secondary school preparation that would enable them to enter a four-year college. She contends that "junior college students are likely to be attracted to a college for practical reasons. . . . They do not seek an intellectual atmosphere, nor do they find it. They tend to see their colleges as placing a relatively low emphasis upon scholarship and a high emphasis on practicality" (p. 49f).

Summary

The two-year college began as a multipurpose institution with a core transfer and preparatory purpose as well as a commitment to occupational, preprofessional, and general education functions. Between 1900 and 1990, these institutions went from being predominantly private to predominantly public and from accommodating a few hundred students to enrolling more than one-half of all entering first-year students in American higher education. Although the rhetoric of the multipurpose or comprehensive institution has not changed, curricula and enrollments have shifted from a predominantly transfer and preparatory emphasis to an increasingly occupational one. The community service offerings of the two-year college, including noncredit, quasi-educational courses, involve, in the 1990s, as many students as the credit programs do. These shifts are embodied in the fact that the two-year college has ceased, for the most part, to identify itself as a junior college, preferring to call itself a community college.

Although the community college leadership has unfailingly endorsed the concept of the multipurpose or comprehensive institution, the literature, the projects, and the national spokespersons for the two-year college have placed primary emphasis on occupational education and community service. The transfer and preparatory function was either taken for granted or considered to need less attention.

At the end of nine decades, junior and community colleges make up an enterprise of 1,250 institutions, mainly public, that enroll an estimated six million credit and six million noncredit students. There are now community colleges in every legislative district and every state. Today, the community college reflects continuity with the past by retaining all the original purposes of the early junior college. It reflects discontinuity in that the core of junior college operation was the transfer and preparatory function while the core of the contemporary community college, in the eyes of many, is not easy to determine.

To the extent that the history of the educational role of the junior and community college has included the liberal arts and transfer functions, it has created a foundation for the collegiate community college. To the extent that the collegiate commitment has been downplayed in the evolution of the community college, that foundation has been constricted. A scrutiny of the history of the educational role of the junior and community college does not sustain the view that the early junior college was exclusively devoted to the liberal arts and transfer purpose. Nor does it support the argument that the history of the educational role can be accurately described as a transition from a preoccupation with the liberal arts and transfer purpose to a preoccupation with terminal vocational education. The situation is more complex, with history reflecting an ongoing commitment to a multipurpose institution and shifting emphases among these purposes.

Chapter Three

Competing Visions
and the Debate over Purpose

This chapter looks to the present. It examines the current educational role of the community college from several perspectives. First, it explores the four major challenges that must be addressed by any community college in the course of carrying out its educational responsibilities. Second, it looks at competing visions or current major interpretations of the educational role as developed by some of the community college's most important friends—Edmund Gleazer, Dale Parnell, and the team of Arthur Cohen and Florence Brawer—asking whether these visions will allow the community college to meet the four major challenges. Third, the chapter concentrates on the major critics of the community college, discussing why they find the institution lacking and describing their respective perceptions regarding its educational role and the four major challenges. Fourth, the chapter looks at some of the fundamental differences between the friends of the community college and its critics, pointing out that much of the dispute between them derives from the different criteria by which each measures community college effectiveness.

These competing visions provide a context for assessing the likelihood of success of a dominant collegiate function. The Cohen-Brawer collegiate-comprehensive vision, as would be expected, emerges as the most viable foundation for building a collegiate institution. The visions of other friends of the community college would place serious constraints on a collegiate commitment. The critics of the community college, on the other hand, play a surprisingly positive role in relation to the collegiate function. In many instances, they urge that the community college *should* function as an effective collegiate institution. Many of their concerns can profitably be addressed by community college leaders who seek to make a stronger commitment to the collegiate role.

Four Challenges

The educational effectiveness of the contemporary community college has depended upon the success with which it deals with four challenges: providing access, sustaining the liberal arts and transfer programs, providing occupational education, and meeting community needs. Other functions of the community college, such as guidance and counseling and maintaining a low-cost operation, are important and support the two-year institution in meeting these challenges. Within the community college enterprise itself, success is generally measured by the extent to which access is available, liberal arts and transfer programs are offered, occupational offerings are scheduled, and community service commitments are made. Success in relation to these challenges is not measured, for the most part, in the form of student learning gains.

Access — the community college's role as democracy's college — was and remains its central and most compelling feature. *Access* refers to the greater availability of the community college to potential students as compared with other higher education institutions. Access may be geographic, financial, academic, or personal. Geographic access is realized when the community college is within commuting distance for students. Financial access is realized when the price of attendance remains comparatively low or at least is not a barrier to attendance for those who are less well off. Academic access is realized when admission to the institution or its programs is open and when attendance is sustained even through periods of poor academic performance. Personal access refers to the comparative convenience of community college offerings — availability of courses, liberal policies for course completion, and use of nontraditional pedagogy such as television courses. Especially in the last twenty-five years, community college leadership has pointed to aggregate enrollment growth as confirmation of the success of its commitment to access. At the heart of this commitment is a powerful belief that the community college's dedication to access is carried out when it functions as a site of opportunity at which effort is highly valued and failure to achieve is not condemned.

To sustain traditional liberal arts and transfer programs, the community college must offer liberal arts or general education coursework that reflects the content and standards required for students to eventually earn the baccalaureate degree. The awarding of associate in arts, associate in science, or associate of general studies degrees is generally viewed as confirmation that this challenge has been successfully met. Additionally, the extent to which students without a degree move from the two-year institution to a baccalaureate institution is an indication of the success of its liberal arts and transfer offerings. The liberal arts constituted the core of early junior college offerings and have consistently been considered to be the community college's major link with other higher education institutions. The success of liberal arts and transfer offerings is not easy to ascertain. Enrollments in these areas have not grown in the past twenty years, there is evidence that expectations of student performance have been reduced, and fewer students have received the associate in arts degree. Evidence about the extent of transfer activity is mixed and trends are not easily discernible (Brint and Karabel, 1989; Cohen and Brawer, 1987, 1989; Lombardi, 1979).

Occupational education, like liberal arts and transfer education, had its origins in the earliest junior colleges. Community college advocates point with pride to the two-year college's ability to provide degree programs in occupational education and to train and retrain workers. These leaders stress the value of the community college in building a paraprofessional work force and participating in job retraining and economic development to meet the country's needs. There is considerable evidence that community colleges have been successful in committing to occupational education: enrollments have grown, acquisition of associate degrees in occupational areas has increased, and economic development programs burgeoned, particularly in the 1980s. Evidence is limited about any positive impact these programs may have on occupational status or job earnings (Pascarella and Terenzini, 1991). Occupational education has become the primary vehicle by which community colleges have justified their existence to local and state officials and the means by which community colleges have developed a special place for themselves in the educational enterprise.

The task of meeting community needs takes many forms in the community college. The fundamental principle undergirding this challenge is that community colleges will shape programs and services based upon their understanding of what is wanted and needed by the local community. In general, community colleges look beyond their traditional credit and degree programs in order to meet community needs. They focus on providing convenient offerings, making facilities available for community use that may or may not be instructional, adding extensive noncredit personal interest courses, showing a commitment to cultural and civic education programs for the community, and providing large numbers of programs that support the educational and training needs of local business and industry, including social services such as child care and job placement. They point to the number of adult students they have served in these off-campus programs. Based on the criterion of providing these services, community colleges have been extraordinarily successful in meeting community needs and establishing themselves as strategic and significant community resources; however, other than by obtaining a general ad hoc response that the community is satisfied, community colleges do not have any mechanisms by which to determine the effectiveness of these efforts.

Friends of the Community College: Advocacy and Vision

More often than not, friends of the community college are partisan, passionate, and partial. Their various conceptions of the community college focus on the positive, and they have limited patience for investigating flaws, weaknesses, or a need for improvement in these institutions. Great pride is appropriately taken in the community college as the ultimate expression of democratic education and as an institution with a fundamental commitment to social equity and equality. The community college is perceived as an extraordinary means by which to realize the traditional American dream of upward mobility, financial success, self-sufficiency, and individual accomplishment. Central to the thinking of the friends of the community college are three premises: (1) these institutions provide educational services that are not otherwise available; (2) without the community college, many more citizens would have been unable to have any higher education at all; and (3) the nation should financially support students' efforts in higher education independent of their success.

Various visions of the community college have been developed, depending on the educational place each leader has advocated for it. Community colleges are considered to be either extensions of the secondary school effort, part of higher education, or neither. All of these views of the community college have been debated since the inception of the early junior college (see Chapter Two). In its most recent form, this discussion has been carried on by four community college leaders: Edmund J. Gleazer, Jr., Dale Parnell, and the team of Arthur Cohen and Florence Brawer. Gleazer does not see the community college as part of either elementary and secondary education or higher education. His vision of the community college is that of a community education center. Parnell places the community college within elementary and secondary education. His vision of the community college concentrates on the importance of terminal occupational education. Cohen and Brawer place the community college in higher education. Their vision concentrates on the community college's liberal arts and transfer role—that is, on collegiate education. Gleazer, Parnell, and Cohen and Brawer emerge as the primary national advocates for these fundamentally different perceptions of the appropriate vision and place of the community college.

The Gleazer Vision: The Community College as a Community Education Center

Gleazer (1968) sees the community college as something more than a junior college. The community college has broader educational functions than its predecessor. For Gleazer, there is a tie between the shift from public to private institutions over the years and the extent to which the two-year school has a community responsibility. He defines the community college's major assignment as the extension of educational opportunity, in contrast to the earlier junior college, in which preparation for a senior institution was paramount. To Gleazer, the transfer and preparatory purpose is not the chief assignment of the community college. Its major task is "to provide those learning experiences commonly needed as the level of educational effort in each community rises two years beyond the high school" (Gleazer, 1968, p. 52).

Gleazer urges community college educators to extend their thinking beyond the bounds of the traditional collegiate environment into which the junior college and the community college were born. He writes about the "community's college," or the community college as a community learning center. In advocating this role, Gleazer downplays the connection of the community college with either elementary and secondary education or traditional collegiate education. He sees the community college as a center for lifelong learning, using the UNESCO definition of lifelong education as being "a process of accomplishing personal, social, and professional development throughout the life-span of individuals in order to enhance the quality of life of both individuals and their collectives. It is a comprehensive and unifying idea which includes formal, non-formal, and informal learning . . . so as to attain the fullest possible development in different stages and domains of life" (pp. 69–70).

In perhaps his most important work on the community college (1980), Gleazer describes its mission as "to encourage and facilitate lifelong learning with community as process and product" (p. 16). Gleazer posits a powerful role for the community in determining the direction of the community college:

"There is really little question about the direction of community college interests. They are directed toward the community. An institution uncertain some years ago whether it was higher or secondary education and where it belonged in the scheme of things, has by and large acknowledged that *the community gives it reason for being*" (my italics) (p. 143).

According to Gleazer, community colleges have been "trapped in tradition" but can go beyond this if they have the capacity to be adaptable, maintain continuing relationships with learners, and are community-oriented. Gleazer argues that community colleges are not, as some might contend, all things to all people if "priority is given to those whose educational options are limited by a variety of circumstances" (p. 8). A community college cannot be a learning system for the entire community. It can become, however, the *nexus*—the bond or link or tie—of a community learning system. Community colleges can function as the means of connection. It is the role of the community college as nexus that places it outside of both the elementary and secondary orbit and that of higher education. Gleazer envisions the community college as a site of evolving policy for lifelong education and as developing a community of learners through a focus on ongoing human development. This would benefit the community as well as individuals and create an awareness of ongoing educational resources for all those who are interested. Gleazer focuses particularly on meeting the personal and social needs of learners in the community.

In looking ahead to the 1980s, Gleazer (1979) emphasizes the need for the community college to stress its role rather than its functions: *"What they will do cannot now be precisely stated. What is needed is an institutional capacity to determine what is appropriate and needful in given circumstances"* (Gleazer's italics) (p. 18). The community college achieves distinction through its cooperative mode. Superior community colleges are adaptable and aware of the community. They sustain continued relationships with the learner, extend opportunity to the unserved, house broadly diverse learners, and have a nexus function.

The Parnell Vision: The Community
College as an Occupational Institution

Dale Parnell is primarily acknowledged for his extraordinary advocacy of occupational education in the community college. In this context, he prefers positioning the community college within the elementary and secondary sector. His powerful support for occupational education is accompanied by a deep suspicion of the tradition liberal arts function in the community college and of the collegiate sector in general. Parnell's community college philosophy is based on four premises. First, community college education is for "ordinary" people, defined by Parnell as those who are neither academically talented nor baccalaureate-bound. In the occupational world, these people, who make up the middle two quartiles of the work force, are not likely to be nuclear scientists, theoretical physicists, or lawyers. They are, in the words of Parnell, "students needing some postsecondary education and training, although not necessarily a baccalaureate degree" (Parnell, 1985b, p. 6).

Second, community college education should be built on a new definition of excellence. Parnell maintains that all education in America is predicated on a single standard that, when applied to higher education, defines excellence in terms of baccalaureate-degree acquisition. He argues for multiple standards of excellence that use a value-added approach to the achievement of the individual student, that is, the student's capacity to develop competencies and proficiencies. Excellence is a variable driven by the diversity of the student population.

Third, community college education should focus on other programs than the baccalaureate for this population of ordinary people. Community college education should be "careers education," which refers to "that delivery system which helps students develop the competencies required to function in the real-life roles of learner, wage earner, citizen, consumer, family member, leisure-time pursuer, and individual" (1985b, p. 65). Parnell sees traditional liberal arts education as the enemy of this educational effort. He views the drive to the baccalaureate as

vitiating efforts to provide excellent education to ordinary people. He believes that the comparatively small percentage of
baccalaureate-degree holders in the current population justifies
deemphasizing baccalaureate-degree acquisition for future gener-
ations. At the same time, he claims to value the liberal arts as
part of a program of careers education — although he devotes
little attention to the content and level of the liberal arts.

Fourth, careers education for ordinary people can most
likely be realized through a revitalized relationship with secondary schools, which Parnell calls the 2 + 2 tech-prep associate-
degree program. The tech-prep model is a liberal-technical educational program for grades 11–14. It is a "middle" program —
seeking middle ground that blends the liberal arts with practical
arts; middle quartiles in the high school population, based on
academic talent and interest; and a midrange of occupations
that call for education beyond high school but not at the level
of the baccalaureate. This view of tech-prep as the primary vehicle for realizing educational excellence for ordinary people
places Parnell in the camp of those who position the community college in the elementary and secondary sector.

Parnell seeks to realize the excellent community college
through an "opportunity with excellence" program that has five
fundamental elements, which constitute articles of faith. He contends that community colleges must be community-based, becoming partners with the communities they serve. They must
be cost-effective, staying within financial reach of potential students and maintaining low operating costs. They must sustain
a caring environment. They must house and encourage com-
petent faculty. And they must be comprehensive, integrating
liberal arts and technical education.

Parnell is also clear about what he rejects. He does not
want to sustain the lack of connection between schooling and
the real world that he believes presently exists, he does not want
a single standard of excellence in education, and he does not
want only one curriculum. He accuses high schools and colleges
of working together to try to force students into "one size of
educational program shoes" — what he calls the college prep/
baccalaureate degree curriculum (Parnell, 1990). He points out

that occupational education has a negative image, which he calls a prestige deficiency. Community colleges, for Parnell, should emphasize employment and economic development, enhancing the quality of life, exemplary practices, lifelong education, community development, access, linkages, and youth services (Parnell, 1981).

The Cohen-Brawer Vision: The Community
College as a Liberal Arts and Transfer Institution

Cohen and Brawer are also friends of the community college, although in a different way than Gleazer and Parnell are. Cohen and Brawer are university researchers rather than community college practitioners. They seek enhancement of the community college and, in the service of progress, they are willing to identify flaws and shortcomings — not to condemn, but to improve. In general, most university researchers see Cohen and Brawer as friends of the community college, whereas many practitioners in the field see them as less friendly and sometimes as adversaries. Cohen and Brawer are the most prolific contributors to the community college literature in the past thirty years. Compared to the work of Parnell and Gleazer, their writings cover a much longer period of time, embrace more aspects of community college life, and rely more extensively on original research. Their fundamental principles about the liberal arts and transfer function have remained consistent over time.

Cohen and Brawer's support of the liberal arts and transfer function does not keep them from supporting the occupational, remedial, and community-based functions of the community college as well. They value and praise its access function, but they are suspicious of the commonly held view of the community college that equates growth in enrollment — generally taken as an indication of effective access — with educational quality. They see the community college as preeminently a place for individual growth and development, yet they question the extent to which it is committed to the traditional notion of student learning — that it consists of cognitive gains made through a sequential curriculum and instruction. In this context, Dougherty (1987) identifies Cohen and Brawer with the functionalist school of community college theoreticians: those who measure the effectiveness of the community college by its contribution to broad access and occupational and income attainment rather than by baccalaureate attainment. He later classifies them among the "collegiate reformers" of the community college because of their desire for a renewed commitment to the transfer function and general academic education (Dougherty, 1991).

Cohen and Brawer, as the primary spokespersons for the collegiate function, have defined this function as "an amalgam of liberal arts curriculum and efforts to promote student transfer" (1987, p. 3). The collegiate function has the greatest impact on general education and transfer programs, but it also affects occupational education programs that include college-level studies. According to their data, approximately 50 percent of enrollments in community colleges are in the humanities, the sciences, the social sciences, mathematics, and fine arts. As Cohen and Brawer see it, the liberal arts in the community college go beyond traditional discipline-based study. They may include any area of coursework in an academically or intellectually defensible area, provided that it does not lead to immediate employment. They describe liberal arts study as basic to societal cohesion. The liberal arts teach the principles of rationality, language, judgment, inquiry, criticism, disciplined creativity, awareness of history, and sensitivity to cultures and the environment.

The liberal arts are also a way of organizing the curriculum. Cohen and Brawer point out that community colleges inherited the liberal arts tradition from the universities and went on to modify it to meet their particular curricular needs. How liberal arts are taught in the community college is affected by the background of the faculty, who may come from either secondary schools or universities. It is also affected by the capacity of students. Cohen and Brawer point to considerable documentation showing that a decline in student abilities resulted, in the 1970s and 1980s, in diminished reading and writing requirements in liberal arts classes. Finally, Cohen and Brawer note that the occupational function has had an impact on liberal arts instruction. One way in which faculty have dealt with students who are focused on immediate employment is by shifting the focus of liberal arts courses from an introduction to an academic discipline to an emphasis on applicability of concepts. This conversion of the liberal arts to a practical discipline is what Cohen and Brawer call general education.

The transfer function, the second aspect of the collegiate function as they define it, refers to what some students do with their liberal arts experience. It describes the flow of students from the community college to a four-year institution or another two-year institution. Cohen and Brawer maintain that the community college's transfer role is equivocal. Transfer makes it possible for students entering higher education through the community college to go on to baccalaureate study and therefore it is a powerful justification for access. It connects the community college with the larger world of higher education. There are negatives, however. The transfer function enables the four-year institution to unduly influence the community college curriculum; and it also encourages an approach to access that may be restrictive depending on the capacity of students for baccalaureate-level success.

Cohen and Brawer's definition of the collegiate function makes the liberal arts and transfer roles central to community college efforts and places the community college squarely in the higher education world. They maintain: "Our position is that the collegiate connection reveals the community college at its finest. These institutions were originally organized around their programs of collegiate studies. . . . this function differentiates these colleges from proprietary trade schools, technical colleges, adult education centers, [and] corporate learning efforts. . . . It is the rudder that keeps the colleges within the mainstream of graded education, stretching from kindergarten to graduate and professional school" (Cohen and Brawer 1987, p. xii). Cohen and Brawer acknowledge that the collegiate function has been at least minimally sustained throughout the history of the junior and community college but would like to see it strengthened.

Earlier, Cohen (1969) argued that the community college lacked an "established educational role," a "sense of self." He maintained that the community colleges were not clear about their effects on students and their contribution to community life. They had not yet developed unique curricula and instructional forms to accomplish their educational tasks and had not yet gained a respected place in American higher education. Cohen said that the community college was not in the business of causing learning; instead, it had four other goals: to perpetuate itself, to offer more and more varied programs, to sustain growth in both enrollments and operating budgets, and to construct buildings.

Ten years later, Cohen (in Vaughan, 1980) sees many of these problems still unresolved. He maintains that there was an almost total collapse of the curriculum in the 1970s and that the literature of the community college reflects a preoccupation with student satisfacation rather than a concern with student learning. Those who write about community colleges "see the colleges only peripherally as educative institutions, choosing instead to view them as agents of transfer payments, of upward mobility for individuals, as shock absorbers for disenfranchised groups demanding entrance to higher education, as recreational and cultural centers for the community, or as credentialing agencies certifying people for employment" (p. 37).

In looking to the future, Cohen and Brawer (1989) identify three trends that must be taken into account in evaluating the effectiveness of the collegiate function to society. First, they maintain that career transfer education, where students use occupational programs for transfer rather than terminal study, is on the increase. Second, what they call diminished linearity, consisting of fewer enrollments in sequences of courses and increased enrollments in courses that are not part of any sequence, is reducing the community college's role in helping students to bridge the first and second years of college study. Third, expansion of enrollments in remedial education are distracting the community college from its college-level responsibilities. These trends and concerns about the institutional identity of the community college need to be addressed if a successful collegiate function is to be realized.

From the Friends' Perspective:
The Effectiveness of the Community College

Whatever the differences of opinion among Gleazer, Parnell, and Cohen and Brawer, they all see the contemporary community college as important, effective, and of profound national value. Their respective visions of the community college are responsive to the four key challenges described at the beginning of this chapter, although there is some variation in the extent to which each vision meets each challenge: Gleazer's primary emphasis is on the community-based challenge, Parnell's is on the occupational challenge, and Cohen and Brawer emphasize the liberal arts and transfer challenge.

Gleazer's vision of the community college increases commitment to access, the first challenge. His community-based learning center provides more varied education in more places, allowing more people to meet their needs, than a traditional institution. Liberal arts and transfer education, the second challenge, is not precluded by Gleazer's approach. Although this area is not strongly emphasized in the community-based model, it would be possible for more learners to avail themselves of this coursework and for the community college, as the focal point of community learning resources, to include traditional educational institutions as part of the learning community. Similarly, occupational education, the third challenge, could continue to play a key role, especially in nontraditional forms of job training, on-site learning experiences, and cooperative education. The final challenge, meeting community needs, is where Gleazer's model is most at home; it responds to this challenge with a full-scale structure and a set of responsibilities for the community college as a nexus institution.

The Parnell vision can be perceived as enhancing access becaues it encourages community college education for those who might otherwise have no collegiate experience at all, but it can also be viewed as discouraging access. Tech-prep might be seen as a way of tracking students into sub-baccalaureate experiences when they might have pursued baccalaureate work.

Parnell contends that only a few students earn the baccalaureate because its acquisition is confined to an elite; this thinking limits access by assuming that the ordinary student is neither interested in nor capable of the baccalaureate experience.

Parnell's vision is at odds with liberal arts and transfer education in several ways. It deemphasizes the community college's connection with four-year work by closely aligning two-year institutions with high schools. By assuming that traditional academic education consisting only of the liberal arts is without practical value, it fails to see liberal arts and transfer education as itself a form of career education, even in the face of increasing evidence that the baccalaureate experience is a form of occupational education. Finally, the tech-prep model fails to clearly define its liberal arts dimension, thus rendering its commitment more rhetorical than genuine.

The Parnell vision strengthens the community college's commitment to occupational education by calling for increased programming in this area. High school populations using the tech-prep model increase enrollments in occupational education, attracting the interest of legislators and perhaps increasing the funding base for occupational programs. Parnell's success in amending the Carl D. Perkins Vocational Education Act in 1990 to include the tech-prep model was considered to be a major gain for community colleges in relation to Congress and the states.

Because the tech-prep approach intimately involves community colleges with area high schools, community-based education stands to gain from the Parnell vision. Spin-offs of technical programs can take place in business and industry and key involvement by employers can occur in the tech-prep programs themselves. Where tech-prep may limit community-based efforts is in its failure to address the large adult population in the community that cannot avail itself of the opportunity being offered.

The Cohen-Brawer vision supports the concept of access, but it suggests more restrictive support than either Parnell's or Gleazer's visions. Parnell and Gleazer believe that the community college must be *academically* convenient — as well as geographically and financially convenient — in order to be accessible. They do not require students wishing to attend a community college to have the cognitive skills needed for college-level work. Within the community college, they are less focused on making academic demands upon students such as college-level reading and writing. Parnell and Gleazer focus more intently on personal development and community improvement than on individual intellectual growth.

Cohen and Brawer do not agree. They do not think it is necessary to lower the academic quality of the community college in order to achieve access. In contrast, they want to retain academic standards *and* bring students to the needed level of academic skill to succeed. Cohen and Brawer want a clear distinction made between college-level and other work. They deplore the dilution of demands on students that they have documented over the past twenty years, believing that access should mean access to a collegiate experience. Other forms of access, such as adult education for personal interest or remedial education, should not blur this fundamental commitment.

Cohen and Brawer strongly support liberal arts and transfer programs. Their emphasis on the importance of a central collegiate function rests primarily on this commitment. However, they also value other aspects of the liberal arts and transfer function in addition to its role of providing the community college's primary connection with the rest of higher education. Cohen and Brawer argue consistently for sequential and structured liberal arts curricula rather than enrollment in isolated courses. They support college-level academic standards in both scope and difficulty of the work expected from students, and they view liberal arts curricula as critical to the development of shared values and social cohesion that is the responsibility of all of higher education.

Cohen and Brawer also strongly support occupational education, understanding the benefits of clearly defined, well-structured, sequential, self-consciously-managed occupational programs. These programs have been among the most effective educational experiences for community college students, who complete these programs, graduate, and go to work. Cohen and Brawer do express the reservation that the occupational function may have become dominant at the price of the collegiate function. They believe that the liberal arts function is the defining value of the community college. At the same time, they urge dismantling of the fire wall between occupational programs and the liberal arts. Students use curricula in such a way that both kinds of courses are taken in many programs, and many occupational experiences are used for transfer purposes — contrary to the conventional wisdom that the transfer program is made up only of the liberal arts.

As with their approach to occupational education, Cohen and Brawer strongly value the community service function of the community college; they are anxious to preserve that function but not use it to blur the commitment to liberal arts and transfer programming. They offer creative suggestions for using community services as a vehicle to expand informal study of the liberal arts (Cohen and Brawer, 1987), and they make suggestions similar to those of Lynne Cheney's later "parallel school" concept (Cheney, 1990), urging that the community college use the community service function as a vehicle to disseminate civic education and culture.

Critics of the Community College

The critics make four points. First, the community college is not "democracy's college": although it is committed to the rhetoric of access and equal opportunity, it really functions to sustain social and economic inequality and therefore is a failed engine of social equality. Second, the community college mainly helps individuals who could have helped themselves: although it contributes to individual growth and development, it is more likely to assist people with higher income and academic ability rather than those with fewer resources and skills. Third, the community college has become a national excuse for failing to deal effectively with mass education: allowing the rhetoric of "democracy's colleges" to dominate the discussion has absolved the rest of higher education from addressing the problem of effective education for the many rather than the few. Fourth, the community college is costly: whether it is measured by the cost per degree recipient—which is high because degree recipients are comparatively few—or by the cost of lost opportunities, the community college is very expensive public policy.

As Grubb stated in 1984, "The claim that the community colleges represent the 'best expression of the egalitarian ideal' rests on two assumptions: that those who attend community colleges would otherwise have received no further education, and that the community college confers on its students an economic advantage over those who do not attend. Both of these propositions may be correct, though evidence for them is far from complete" (p. 44ff). Subsequent reserach (Grubb, 1989, 1992; Lee, 1992; Pascarella and Terenzini, 1991) has yet to provide this evidence.

The Community College
as a Failed Engine of Social Equality

Part of the folklore of American society is the notion that education is a critical resource in the struggle of the individual to achieve his or her career and personal goals. It is through education, the nation claims to believe, that individuals overcome poverty, achieve economic and social success, and move ahead. Education is a powerful mechanism for increasing opportunity. Critics of the community college maintain that, of all the higher education institutions in the country, the community college should do the most to ensure the realization of opportunity through education and has accomplished the least. The critics therefore are repeating the claims made by community college educators themselves and are asking if there is adequate evidence to support these claims.

The Cooling-Out Function. One camp of critics, indebted to Burton Clark (1960a, 1960b, 1980), argues that if community colleges were successful, the society would see significant changes in the socioeconomic status of the lower-income, minority, and female populations of these institutions. Evidence should demonstrate that the millions of students who have attended community colleges—or at least a large number of them—

experience changes in income level and occupation. That evidence is not there. To the contrary, these critics find that the community college not only fails to assist in the upward economic mobility of the population it serves, but actually functions to prevent it.

Although Clark is the first to advance the argument that community colleges can function to prevent upward mobility, he does not characterize this as a negative feature of these institutions. Those who have built upon Clark's argument (Dougherty, 1987; Karabel, 1972; Pincus, 1980; Zwerling, 1976) go beyond his analysis to offer negative judgments about the role of the community college. Clark himself sees community colleges as contributing to a system of higher education in which commitments to democracy and selectivity are both maintained. He says, "The innovation of the junior college in performing the cooling-out function is providing structured alternatives" (1960b, p. 163).

Basing his arguments on a single case study, that of San Jose Junior College in San Jose, California, in the 1950s, Clark maintains that community colleges have three functions: (1) they extend education to those for whom it was not formerly available, (2) they function as a screening agent for those who go on to the baccalaureate, and (3) they perform the cooling-out function. It is this last role description that has produced considerable consternation among community college advocates. Clark's phrase, "cooling-out function," has become synonymous with criticism of the community college as a failed engine of social and economic mobility, although this is not a position taken by Clark in his book (Clark, 1960b).

The cooling-out function serves to shift students of limited academic talent from pursuit of a baccalaureate program to an "undesired destination," a terminal education program. Clark calls them "latent terminal" students. Community college educators encourage this shift, as some later critics argue, not because of institutional complicity in preserving socioeconomic inequality but because, in their eyes, it is preferable to having students drop out or otherwise fail to complete a program. As Clark puts it, "Since the movement of students in the college must be principally away from the transfer work, the efficacy of the college is especially defined by its ability to reassign the student from a transfer to a terminal major without losing him in the process" (1960b, p. 146f). Clark calls this the "structured failure" role of the community college. The result is that the latent terminal student, one who aspires to transfer to another college to complete four years, is destined never to get beyond the community college.

The cooling-out function results from what Clark calls a broad disjunction between ends and means in education. This disjunction is the result of several factors in our society: an emphasis on individual achievement that manifests itself in pressing on through education, a perception of college education as the main road to upward mobility, and a belief in equal rights in education that would allow everyone to enter college. Our democratic ethos sets personal ends, but the standards of education control the means. The disjunction between means and ends is the disjunction between the open door and standards. Students may enter, but the standards of higher education may prevent them from reaching their desired destination.

Karabel, Zwerling, Pincus and Grubb, and Dougherty. Clark's notion of the community college experience as one of "structured failure," at least for some students, became the foundation for the work of a number of community college critics. Clark was content to formulate but not judge the cooling-out function; he refers to it at one point as a situation of failure in which those responsible are acting in good faith (1960b, p. 160). In contrast, scholars such as Fred Pincus, Kevin Dougherty, Norton Grubb, and L. Steven Zwerling, led by Jerome Karabel's seminal critiques of the community college, combine Clark's concept with their concerns that community colleges are producing socioeconomic effects that reproduce social inequality. They have built a modest but significant body of commentary on the community college as an institution that deliberately misleads students and the nation. Community colleges promise upward mobility through education while remaining fully aware that the educational experiences they offer are most likely to produce just the opposite effect. Because of this, community college educators are consciously sustaining inequality and inequity. According to Karabel (1972):

Despite the idealism and vigor of the community
college movement, there has been a sharp contra-
diction between official rhetoric and social reality.
Hailed as the "democratizers of higher education,"
community colleges are, in reality, a vital component of the class-based tracking system. The model
junior college student, though aspiring to a four-
year diploma upon entrance, receives neither an
associate nor a bachelor's degree. The likelihood
of his persisting in higher education is *negatively* influenced by attending a community college. . . .
Having increased access to higher education, community colleges are notably unsuccessful in retaining their students and in reducing class differen-
tials in educational opportunity [p. 555].

Karabel first questions the fundamental commitment of
the community college, asking whether any single institution
can deliver — as well as promise — access *and* achievement. He
suggests that two institutions can accomplish this, but not one.
Karabel (1974) then focuses on the shift within the community college from offering mainly college-parallel liberal arts
programs to emphasizing terminal occupational programs. He
sees this as a response to the enormous demand for technical
and professional workers between 1950 and 1970. Karabel says,
however, that student demand did not warrant this shift, and
he identifies a number of "sponsors" of the occupational emphasis: community college administrators who seek a unique niche
atop a vocational education hierarchy in higher education; the
business community, which wants occupational training at public expense; foundations; the Carnegie Commission of Higher
Education; organizations such as the American Association of
Community Colleges (AACC) and the ACE; the general academic community; and the federal government, which in the
1963 Vocational Educational Act supported postsecondary technical training *distinct from* baccalaureate education and in 1972
supported Higher Education Act amendments that authorized
$850 million dollars over three years for postsecondary *occupa-
tional* education.

The vocationalizing of the community college has, in Karabel's view, reinforced the reproduction of social inequality to which he believes the community college is already dedicated. Studies indicate that, contrary to community college claims, occupational education does not lead to upward mobility and economic security. Occupational programs do not outrank liberal arts programs in economic returns or quality of students. The expansion of occupational programs came about, he contends, at the expense of the transfer function. This, to Karabel, means that community colleges are cut off from the mainstream of higher education. He identifies the "fate of their increasingly precarious academic transfer programs" as the major dilemma facing community colleges (Karabel, 1986), and he warns, "In a society in which professional and managerial jobs are increasingly monopolized by college graduates, we should know clearly what a weakening of linkages with four-year colleges really means: a cutting off of opportunities for long-range upward mobility for those students, already disproportionately lacking in cultural and economic resources, who are enrolled in higher education's bottom track" (Zwerling, 1986, p. 27).

Karabel is not optimistic about the community college. He does offer some suggestions that may help it to shift away from its role in reproducing social inequality. First, it is important to distinguish between equality and equality of opportunity. The *potential* for equality of condition is different from *actual* equality. Community colleges have confused their investment in equality of opportunity with commitment to genuine social equality. Second, community colleges should attend more conscientiously to the transfer function (Zwerling, 1986). On the negative side, Karabel suggests that tracking in higher education will become more rigid. Community colleges will enroll more lower-status students, occupational education will become more pervasive, and community colleges will emphasize terminal education over the transfer function. Karabel questions the community college's ability to overcome the current class structure and asks whether putting more money in the community colleges, transforming them into four-year schools, or vocationalizing them will be of value. He sees the community college as continuing to function in an ambiguous role, remaining an educational environment that promises opportunity but delivers results for only a few—with attrition and lack of educational and economic attainment the fate of most students.

Zwerling (1976) continues the discussion initiated by Karabel in 1972. He is especially concerned about the impact of the community college on social equality and questions the strategies employed by the community colleges to achieve this goal. Zwerling characterizes those who support the community college as having a "meritocratic" view, in which they believe that the goal of education is to maximize individual potential. According to this view, individuals are fully able to take advantage of educational opportunities; the community college, an institution devoted to expansion of the opportunity base, contributes to the development of this potential. Zwerling contrasts this with his own view, a "revisionist" position. For Zwerling, the real goal of the community college is to maintain the current social and economic structure and not to help the individual. As Zwerling sees it, only a few are likely to benefit from the opportunity the community college claims it offers to everyone.

Zwerling argues that social reform is needed before genuine educational opportunity can occur. The class-serving nature of American higher education can be changed if students are "heated up"—become angry about what is happening. They need to realize that the "people's college" does not serve the people, but only provides an illusion of upward mobility, and that mass higher education does not produce upward mobility and a more equal society. He points out that students in community colleges come from the lowest socioeconomic classes and have the highest dropout rate of any college population. Zwerling, at least in 1976, would eliminate the community college in the name of building a less hierarchical society, describing the community college as "the most class-serving of educational institutions" (p. 251). He would send community college students to four-year schools and raises the issue of establishing four-year community colleges.

Zwerling's thinking has not changed significantly over the years. In 1986 he maintains that the democratization of education has not produced greater social equity, saying that inequality of income has not diminished and schooling has been used to sanction this inequality as being fair to all.

Pincus (1974, 1980) and Grubb (1984, 1988, 1992) concentrate on the community college's claims about occupational education. Pincus shares Clark's view that the community college performs the cooling-out function and Karabel's perception that it reproduces social inequality. He provides significant evidence that occupational education and its advocacy by community college educators strongly support Karabel's perception of the community college. Pincus contends that, contrary to the claims made by community colleges, the economic benefits of occupational education are modest and a "substantial minority" of students do not get jobs in the fields in which they are trained. He argues that occupational graduates do not have better employment rates than college graduates and that we know little about the relative incomes of occupational and college graduates. Pincus's research on the limited and equivocal impact of occupational education on economic and educational attainment does two things: it undermines the community college's claim that occupational education leads to economic security and social mobility and it suggests that occupational education in the community college is part of a tracking system that "reproduces and legitimates the social and economic inequalities that are endemic in a capitalistic society" (1980, p. 354). He does not take up solutions to these difficulties.

Grubb questions whether the community college provides students with the kind of occupational education — aside from transfer — that they need to be successful. He points out that the community college is not sustaining enrollment in the occupational programs that are responsive to economic conditions and the changing labor market. To the contrary, the community college's occupational education programs have become relatively independent of the labor markets they are intended to serve. Grubb maintains that the community college has failed to establish a rational relationship between education and work. For example, the development of occupational education in the 1980s showed a preoccupation with high-technology jobs, even though the available evidence pointed to job growth in other, less glamorous areas.

Dougherty (1987, 1991, 1992) argues in a similar vein when he looks at baccalaureate-degree attainment. For him, the community college reproduces social inequality, particularly through its negative impact on baccalaureate-degree attainment. He states: "Generally, baccalaureate aspirants entering community colleges secure significantly fewer bacherlor's degrees, fewer years of education, less prestigious jobs, and in the long run, poorer paying jobs than comparable students entering four-year colleges" (1987, p. 99f). He does acknowledge that the community college may be beneficial for occupational students, but notes that thus far the data are neither consistent nor conclusive. In a later treatment of the subject, Dougherty (1991) argues that this negative impact on baccalaureate-bound students is an institutional effect. It cannot be attributed solely to the community college student's poorer academic preparation or less advantaged background.

Dougherty concludes that community colleges are less able than four-year institutions to aid in educational and economic attainment. He calls for more research on the effects of attendance at colleges and offers several structural options for the community college in the future (see Chapter Seven).

Is There Really a Diverted Dream? The Diverted Dream (Brint and Karabel, 1989) is perhaps the most ambitious effort to date to examine the community college as well as the most comprehensive undertaking by its critics. It is part history, part sociology, and part public policy. The book continues Karabel's criticism of the community college articulated in 1972. Brint and Karabel build on a combination of Clark's work and their expectation that the community college's commitment to access is truly intended to diminish social and economic inequality. They see the junior or community college as initially being founded with two intents: to relieve universities of the responsibility of educating lower-division students and to provide an alternative educational vehicle for these students. These intents were carried out through the establishment of two-year institutions that initially were private, focused primarily on liberal arts education, and legally connected to secondary school systems. Over the years, junior colleges grew in number and size, became increasingly public rather than private, and expanded their educational role through an increased emphasis on occupational and community-based education, as the shift from junior to community colleges suggests.

Brint and Karabel hold the community college accountable for its claim to provide educational opportunity to a hitherto unprecedented extent in the society. But where community college educators use one criterion to justify their claim to be the premier access institution in American higher education, Brint and Karabel use another. Community college advocates have invariably pointed to *participation* as the supreme test of their effectiveness as access institutions. Brint and Karabel maintain that participation is not enough; *achievement* should be the fundamental test. They examine the community college, using a number of achievement indicators such as associate-degree completion, baccalaureate-degree completion, and earnings after graduation, and conclude that the institution does not live up to its claims.

This ineffectiveness does not hold true for all students. Brint and Karabel acknowledge that many students achieve educational and economic gains that would not have been realized without the community college. But when *aggregate* numbers of students are examined, the failure of the community college can be seen. In general, community college students do not make the gains in education and economic status characteristic of students entering four-year institutions.

Brint and Karabel go beyond this documentation of the community college's limitations to make two other key points. First, they maintain that the primary reason for the community college's inability to better assist students is its emphasis on terminal occupational education. This emphasis did not come from any thorough documentation of student demand or from a clear indication of need from government or the business community. Instead, it resulted from the preference of a few community college leaders who sought to find a unique place for the institution in American higher education. Because there was no competition in the two-year terminal occupational niche, the community colleges moved in.

Second, by emphasizing terminal occupational education in the absence of significant need, community colleges, intentionally or not, aligned themselves with the social forces that work against educational and economic mobility. For a long time, community colleges have housed more students of lower socioeconomic status than other educational institutions. By focusing on less ambitious educational and economic goals for poorer students, who are more likely than their four-year counterparts to be racial minorities or women, community colleges have not contributed to upward mobility in society, but instead have discouraged it. Brint and Karabel claim that community colleges reproduce social inequality through their insistence on terminal occupational education and their concomitant refusal to sustain strong connections with the higher education enterprise for the students who need it most.

The community college world reacted to Brint and Karabel's statements with a combination of disbelief, anger, and denial. Brint and Karabel were taken to task for what was seen as a lack of understanding of the community college and hostility toward it. They were accused of attempting to undermine the worthy work of the community college and destroying access. In addition, they were criticized for their use — or misuse — of data and charged with failure to argue adequately for their hypothesis. These various reactions highlighted the radically different standards of judgment used by most community college educators on the one hand and by Brint and Karabel on the other. Again, community colleges defined their responsibility toward access in terms of how many students attempted an educational experience. Although they provided extensive student and academic support services, these institutions could not ensure student achievement and separated responsibility for achievement from responsibility to provide access. Opportunity and participation defined the community college's responsibility toward upward mobility. Brint and Karabel, on the other hand, evaluated responsibility toward access in terms of its impact, asking what educational and economic gains the community college had produced for its student population. For Brint and Karabel, achievement defines the community college's responsibility to increase upward mobility.

Although the Brint-Karabel thesis is a powerful one and requires serious attention, community college educators might raise a number of legitimate concerns to challenge it. Brint and Karabel do not provide strong evidence for their contention that the emphasis on terminal occupational education was the result of the impact of the national leadership on individual institutions. They do not establish a causal relationship between the preferences of national leadership and institutional decision making and shifts to occupational programming. More information is needed to avoid being left with only a vague notion that national organizations influence college campuses; the process by which national leadership controls individual institutions is not made clear.

Second, Brint and Karabel's contention that community colleges reproduce social inequality through occupational education is open to challenge on several fronts. In terms of intent, the community college's commitment to upward mobility has always been couched in terms of individual gain rather than the gains of the entire student population. The rhetoric speaks to the societal benefits that are obtained when many *individuals* are successful. The community college's focus has been on individual students and, over time, their impact on social classes. Brint and Karabel demand that community colleges do what few social institutions — educational or otherwise — have ever done: produce a major change in the socioeconomic status of an entire group in a single generation. Their demands for upward mobility appear unreasonable.

Third, their extensive discussion of the way social inequality is reinforced through emphasis on terminal occupational education strongly suggests that this was a deliberately sought-after goal of the community college. Brint and Karabel are part of the school of socioeconomic thought that divides society into victims and oppressors. In the case of the community college, its leadership is the alleged oppressor and its students are the alleged victims. This interpretation fails for lack of evidence and can be treated only as a theoretical framework in which to consider the subject. But even as a framework, it is highly pejorative.

Fourth, the concept of terminal occupational education is blurred. As Brint and Karabel themselves will admit, the definition of occupational programming has varied over time and sometimes even overlaps with that of the liberal arts and transfer function. Further, Brint and Karabel do not clarify whether the real problem, as they see it, is vocational education or *terminal* vocational education. They also acknowledge that occupational education itself constitutes a hierarchy that results in differential gains for students. This means that Brint and Karabel's prime culprit in the community college's reproduction of inequality — occupational education — is not clearly defined.

Fifth, the effects of enrollment in a community college cannot be conclusively determined. Whether or not community colleges contribute to enhanced occupational status or increased earnings is not clear (Adelman, 1992; Pascarella and Terenzini, 1991). In the face of equivocal data, Brint and Karabel's claim that an occupational focus is deleterious becomes suspect.

Nonetheless, Brint and Karabel have provided the most profound treatment of the contemporary community college that has been undertaken in the history of this enterprise. Their work may be construed as advocacy for a vision of the community college as an institution that must either sustain strong ties with higher education enterprise or diminish its claim to a major role in the production of upward mobility, even for individuals. Their concerns about the limited educational and economic advancement of community college students are legitimate in light of the low socioeconomic status of these students; community colleges should use Brint and Karabel's analysis as a basis for reconsidering their programming, standards, and mission. Brint and Karabel call attention to the critical social role of the community college and the educational experiences that must be available if that role is to be realized.

Are the Critics Right?

The critics are right in some of what they say. Measured by educational attainment, occupational status, and earnings, the community college does not produce much for its students. Students beginning higher education in the community college are less likely to earn the baccalaureate than those starting out in a four-year school. Those who earn the baccalaureate resemble their counterparts in four-year schools more closely than other students in the community college: they come from more affluent backgrounds and have experienced greater academic success prior to coming to the community college. Data on the occupational status and earnings of community college students are equivocal, failing to support the claim that the community college produces economic gains for its students. Community colleges ~perience high attrition, and degree recipients constitute a small ~entage of their student population.

The critics, however, are wrong to the extent that they idence for some of their other contentions. Their major tions are that the community college is a vocationalized titution, that community colleges systematically and intentionally set out to preserve social inequality, and that their leadership ignores the desires of students who continue to show interest in the liberal arts and transfer function, as well as ignoring data confirming the educational and economic advantages of the baccalaureate over the associate degree. These contentions can be treated with interest, but, in the face of limited evidence, they cannot be considered as accurate descriptions of the community college experience.

Finally, many community college educators argue that the critics are wrong because they have chosen the wrong criteria and have been satisfied to judge the institution with inadequate evidence. The critics focus on educational attainment; the community college educators focus on educational opportunity. The critics believe that they have confirmed the limited educational gains to be made through the community college, whereas community college educators disagree, finding the evidence incomplete and misleading. The critics use certain theoretical constructs in their discussions of social equality, the relationship between educational leadership and educational institutions, and the economic role of education in society; community college educators challenge the viability of these theoretical frameworks.

From the Critics' Perspective:
The Effectiveness of the Community College

The earlier discussion of whether or not the community college "works" from the perspectives of various community college advocates concluded that if the effectiveness of the community college was measured by its ability to ensure access, sustain liberal arts and transfer programs, provide occupational education, and offer community-based education, the community college indeed does work. The advocates, however, are reasonably content with the investment that the community college makes as distinct from the results it produces. They focus more on offerings and intentions than on their impact and offer a limited assessme effects. Not so with the critics.

With regard to access, all the critics agree that th munity college has been successful in ensuring large enr and participation. They also agree, however, that with th ception of some occupational programs, the community colleg is not a successful access institution when access is measured by criteria that include achievement. The fundamental difference of opinion between critics and advocates requires a major public policy discussion, which community colleges should lead. With the exception of the community college, sanctioning of the higher education enterprise comes when it produces results: graduates, degrees, or research. The enterprise is considered effective only to the extent that it produces. Attrition, dropouts, and marginal degree-acquisition rates are all considered indicative of a problem within higher education. In contrast to this attitude, community college educators, emphasizing opportunity, seek sanction for the educational experience whether or not it produces results in the form of graduates and degrees. They consider themselves to be effective when students try, not when they try *and* succeed. This difference in defining success is fundamental to the way critics and advocates assess the future role of the community college.

Most of the critics consider the liberal arts and transfer role to be the major failure to date of the community college. Some critics point to the community college's limitations in serving minorities and low-income students; others point to its inability to sustain college-level standards across all progams. The critics base their contention primarily on analyses of persistence and degree acquisition in the community college. They reason that if the community college were successful in sustaining liberal arts and transfer programs, more students would persist, more would obtain the associate degree, and more would go on to earn the baccalaureate. The critics have not, however, examined the effectiveness of these programs based on other indicators of achievement. They do not, for example, study the intellectual development of students in liberal arts and transfer programs. For the most part, they are content with proxies such as number of degrees or ability to transfer.

There is some agreement among critics that community college can be successful in offering occupational education; a few students do realize economic, occupational, and social gains. Certainly community colleges are more effective in this area than in dealing with liberal arts and transfer programs. Nonetheless, serious problems have been identified. Occupational education does not produce the economic gains for students that community colleges advertise. Students may be encouraged into occupational programs for which there is limited demand, and community colleges may use occupational education to discourage students from more academically ambitious goals. Community colleges have participated in developing the perception that some occupations require the associate degree, which will produce economic gains beyond the level that can be realized with only a high school education — and this is not always true. They have sometimes used occupational education as a "wedge" issue to separate themselves and their students from traditional higher education, which may work to the students' detriment. Although the occupational function of the community college works at times, in the eyes of the critics, the price is very high for students and society.

The critics infrequently address the issue of the community-based function, but they also agree that it is successful. Community colleges have, for years, enrolled large numbers of people from the community in a range of both credit and noncredit courses. These institutions also deal effectively with the needs of business and industry. They provide services to their districts that go well beyond their basic instructional function. Zwerling (1986) is the exception here, noting that the continuing education function of the community college, like the other community college functions, may also contribute to social inequality.

The critics question the extent to which the community-based function can be the mainstay of the community college as well as the extent to which it interferes with other functions. Limited public support is available for community-based services, as indicated by the public's lack of willingness to fund them the way they fund traditional programs. The critics also raise questions about the impact of community-based programs on the community college's mission. These programs may encourage confusion about the commitment of the institution by further diversifying institutional energy. The community-based function casts the community college in the role of an educational service center and further removes it from its historical collegiate base. Finally, community-based efforts that are also occupational may turn community colleges into devices of business and industry or publicly supported occupational training centers for the private sector—a role that is questioned as an appropriate use of public funds.

Has the contemporary community college worked? In the eyes of its critics, not very well. Its limited success is largely confined to occuptional education and community-based services at the expense of the collegiate function. Its commitment to access appears rhetorical and shallow because it places too little emphasis on achievement and results. If some of the critics seem harsh when they portray the community college as an educational hoax, an unfulfilled promise, or a revolving door, some of the advocates appear naive in their contentment with only the availability of educational opportunity and their apparent lack of concern for the effects of the community college on society.

Summary

The competing visions of the contemporary community college and the work of its critics, an amalgam of support and concern for the two-year institution, make it clear that a decision for the collegiate community college requires controversial choices among the important values that have guided these institutions. The friends of the community college share a dedication to access and participation. Even acknowledging the differences among the Gleazer, Parnell, and Cohen-Brawer visions, they are nonetheless united in their powerful commitment to the community college as a crucial site of educational opportunity. A strong collegiate function would strain this union, however. While the Cohen-Brawer vision of this opportunity is the most conducive to establishing a strong collegiate commitment, neither Gleazer nor Parnell can easily accommodate this role for the community college.

Whether the critics are examining the community college's occupational commitment or its support for liberal arts, they all share the conclusion that the community college is a site of limited educational attainment. They might applaud the effort to establish a dominant collegiate function, but they would likely remain skeptical about the likelihood of its success. Yet the critics, with their emphasis on educational attainment, articulate a challenge for the collegiate community college that is a foundation on which it can build strong and effective programs.

The respective positions of the friends and critics of the community college cannot be reconciled. These two groups start from very different assumptions about how to evaluate the community college. The friends focus on the educational gains for students and society that would not exist if there were no community colleges. No matter how limited the gains are, they see them as the primary justification that the community college works. The critics, on the other hand, focus on the educational gains that they believe ought to be the result of a community college education—eventual baccalaureate-degree attainment and improved occupational status and earnings. To the extent that these gains are not produced, they condemn the community college.

Over and over, since 1900, one question has remained unanswered for these institutions: how can any educational institution marry the inclusionary principle of opportunity with the exclusionary principle of excellence? Selective four-year institutions and universities are not confronted with this dilemma. They do not make extensive inclusionary claims that lead to open-door admissions. Elementary and secondary education also avoid this dilemma. They are precluded by law from making exclusionary claims. Indeed, as Karabel suggests, access and achievement may not be realizable in a single institution. The access-achievement, or opportunity-excellence, dilemma is also a metaphor for the friends-critics debate. To date, the community college enterprise has enshrined the dilemma, not resolved it. "Opportunity with Excellence" is the official motto of the AACC. The AACC would benefit its members by leading a serious national debate and discussion exploring this difficult issue.

Chapter Four

The Current Status of Collegiate Education

This chapter examines the current status of the collegiate function in the community college. It describes curricular offerings and enrollments in the liberal arts during the past fifteen years, reviews the current state of non–liberal arts enrollments, and explores presidential attitudes toward the curriculum. This examination provides information about two of the four conditions community colleges must meet to be collegiate: whether the liberal arts and career education are the majority of offerings, and whether the needed institutional valuing of these curricula is provided at least by the institution's chief executive officer.

Two major findings result from this examination. First, the curriculum of the community college provides an adequate although somewhat weak foundation on which to build a dominant collegiate function. Second, community college presidents play an important but too limited role in developing curricula and thus building collegiate values in their institutions. The potential for a powerful collegiate function is present within the community college, but it will take serious, long-term, and energetic leadership to ensure its success.

The information presented here on curriculum and enrollment is based on the Total Community College Curriculum Study, conducted by the Center for the Study of Community Colleges (CSCC) during 1991 and 1992 (Cohen and Ignash, 1993). The discussion of presidential attitudes is based on a national survey of community college presidents and curricula conducted in 1991 by the National Center for Academic Achievement and Transfer of the American Council on Education with the assistance of the CSCC.

Curriculum and Enrollment

In 1991, the CSCC examined enrollments in various curricula in 164 two-year institutions. They compared liberal arts enrollments by section with similar studies during the past fifteen years (Cohen and Ignash, 1993). They then moved on to assess non-liberal arts enrollments and non–liberal arts transfer to four-year institutions.

There have been six CSCC studies of liberal arts curricula since 1975, which provide a basis for comparison and evaluation of the state of the liberal arts in the community college at the beginning of the 1990s. The 164 institutions in the 1991 study are a sufficiently representative group of community colleges and the results can reasonably be compared with those of earlier studies.

The 164 institutions in the 1991 study were identified in part because of their participation in The Ford Foundation–sponsored work of the CSCC and the National Center for Academic Achievement and Transfer in Washington, D.C., which was designed to strengthen the transfer function in the community college. All institutions in the study were public with the exception of 10 private or Native American–controlled institutions. Forty-eight institutions enrolled fewer than 1,500 students, 55 institutions enrolled 1,500 to 6,000 students, and 61 institutions enrolled more than 6,000 students. College catalogs and Spring 1991 course schedules were collected from each institution and class sections were analyzed to determine enrollment counts.

The first part of the survey focused on the liberal arts. The 164 institutions offered a total of 104,565 sections of all courses. Of these, 56.6 percent, or 59,205, were in the liberal arts. The liberal arts were divided into six major disciplines:

humanities, English, fine and performing arts, social sciences, sciences, and mathematics and computer sciences. The sections were then coded and tallied. In order to determine the level of proficiency required by the courses, they were divided into the categories of "remedial" (carrying no credit), "standard" (offering credit but with no prerequisites), and "advanced" (offering credit and having prerequisites). Either standard or advanced courses could be considered transferable, or college-level. To say that course content is transferable, however, does not take into account whether or not college-level expectations of student performance have been established by the faculty.

The curriculum study indicates that, in general, liberal arts enrollments expanded slightly during the previous five years, from 52 percent in 1986 to 56.6 percent in 1991. A few subject areas showed increases or decreases in enrollments. English, foreign languages, and political science enrollments grew, while engineering, fine and performing arts, and mathematics enrollments declined. Anthropology, environment, music appreciation, and interdisciplinary humanities and social science courses made up the smallest enrollments in the liberal arts and showed little change (see Table 4.1).

The study shows that 80 percent of the humanities coursework is standard with regard to level of proficiency, except for foreign languages and literature. In English, more than 30 percent of courses are remedial and approximately 20 percent are advanced. In the sciences, social sciences, and fine and performing arts, almost all coursework is standard or advanced. In mathematics and computer sciences, as with English, a significant percentage (15.9 percent) of coursework is remedial (see Table 4.2). The standard level of the major disciplines predominates in all institutions participating in the survey; 83 to 100 percent of institutions offer these courses. Similarly, 59 to 87 percent of the institutions offer the advanced level of instruction. Eighty-nine percent of institutions offer remedial English and 65 percent offer remedial math (see Table 4.3).

The second part of the study focused on the remaining portion of the credit curriculum, which was designated non-liberal arts. The study identified 45,360 of the 104,565 sections,

Table 4.1. Percentage of Sections in Community College
Liberal Arts Classes by Broad Subject Area, 1986[a] and 1991.[b]

Subject Area	1986	1991
Agriculture	1.2	0.1
Anthropology	0.6	0.8
Art history	1.0	1.0
Biology	5.0	5.3
Chemistry	3.0	2.3
Earth and space	1.0	1.1
Economics	2.5	2.2
Engineering	5.0	2.5
English	21.0	22.5
Environment	0.2	0.1
Fine and performing arts	13.0	9.6
Foreign languages	5.0	8.5
History	4.0	4.8
Integrated sciences	N.A.	0.6
Interdisciplinary humanities	0.1	1.0
Interdisciplinary social sciences	0.1	0.9
Literature	2.0	1.9
Mathematics	20.0	18.9
Music appreciation	0.8	0.8
Philosophy	1.0	1.8
Physics	2.0	1.6
Political science	2.0	3.0
Psychology	6.0	5.4
Sociology	3.0	2.9

[a]$N = 99$ colleges. [b]$N = 164$ colleges.
Source: Center for the Study of Community Colleges, "Total Community College
Curriculum Study 1991," in Cohen and Ignash, 1993.

or 43.4 percent, as "non-liberal arts." The categories developed
by the CSCC for this study were Agriculture, Business and
Office, Marketing and Distribution, Health, Home Economics,
Technical Education, Engineering and Technology, Trade and
Industry, Personal Skills and Avocational Courses, Education,
and Other. The taxonomy was based mainly on the major categories used by the National Center for Research in Vocational
Education at the University of California, Berkeley. Transferable non-liberal arts courses constitute the career education
coursework that is essential for a dominant collegiate function.

Among the 164 colleges in the study, four areas accounted
for more than 80 percent of the sections: Business and Office,

Table 4.2. Percentage of Remedial, Standard,
and Advanced Courses in Each Major Discipline Area.

Discipline	Remedial	Standard	Advanced
Humanities	0.1	82.5	17.4
English	30.5	49.7	19.8
Fine and performing arts	0.0	62.8	37.2
Social science	0.0	85.8	14.2
Science	1.0	67.6	31.7
Math and computer sciences	15.9[a]	62.2	21.9

[a]Self-paced, individualized, and lab courses were not counted. It is likely that a large number of remedial math courses were self-paced, individualized, and lab courses, which would explain the low remedial math percentage.
Source: Center for the Study of Community Colleges, "Total Community College Curriculum Study 1991," in Cohen and Ignash, 1993.

Table 4.3. Percentage of Colleges Providing Remedial, Standard,
and Advanced Courses in the Six Major Discipline Areas.

Discipline	Remedial	Standard	Advanced
Humanities	1	97	80
English	89	99	84
Fine and performing arts	0	83	75
Social science	0	98	59
Science	5	100	87
Math and computer sciences	65	98	86

Source: Center for the Study of Community Colleges, "Total Community College Curriculum Study 1991," in Cohen and Ignash, 1993.

Technical Education, Trade and Industry, and Personal Skills (see Table 4.4). Business and Office included accounting, business and management, secretarial, labor law, and other business studies. Technical Education included computer software applications; fire, police, and law enforcement; journalism, graphics, and photo journalism. Trade and Industry included construction, automotive, the hospitality industry, computer-aided design and manufacturing, welding, and apparel construction. Personal Skills included physical education, first-year orientation, introduction to the library, parenting, and career and life planning.

Table 4.4. Number of Sections Offered and
Percentage of Non–Liberal Arts Courses in U.S. Colleges.[a]

Subject	No. of Course Sections	% of Non–Liberal Arts Courses
Agriculture	529	1.2
Business and Office	11,156	24.6
Marketing and Distribution	1,524	3.4
Health	4,629	10.2
Home Economics	106	0.2
Technical Education	8,233	18.2
Engineering and Technology	889	2.0
Trade and Industry	8,427	18.6
Personal Skills and Avocational Courses	8,643	19.1
Education	1,147	2.5
Other	77	0.2
Total all subjects	45,360	

[a]$N = 164$.
Source: Center for the Study of Community Colleges, "Total Community College Curriculum Study 1991," in Cohen and Ignash, 1993.

A key question about the dominant collegiate function is the extent to which non–liberal arts sections are transferable to four-year institutions. This question cannot be answered, however, with a generalization that encompasses all the institutions in the study. The study indicates that non–liberal arts transfer is more heavily dependent upon the receiving institution than liberal arts transfer. Although liberal arts transfer frequently involves discipline-based introductory courses that are common to most colleges and universities, non–liberal arts offerings do not have a comparable core. Transfer is a function not only of college-level complexity in tasks (see Chapter Six), but also of whether the subject matter that is offered is available at the four-year institution.

Two kinds of receiving institutions were involved in the study—research universities and comprehensive colleges. These receiving institutions vary in two ways: (1) they house significantly different kinds of offerings in the non–liberal arts at the lower-division level and (2) they differ greatly in the number of courses and programs they offer in non–liberal arts. Both of these factors have a significant impact on the acceptance of non-liberal arts courses by four-year institutions. Even within each category of receiving institution — the research university or the comprehensive college — the non-liberal arts courses that transfer and the extensiveness of the transfer vary considerably.

The study concentrated on five states to obtain data on non-liberal arts transfers: California, Florida, Illinois, North Carolina, and Texas. These data do not permit valid generalizations about non-liberal arts transfer throughout the country. The study itself, however, is a model for state inquiry into non-liberal arts transfer and the relationship of a state's community colleges to its four-year institutions. Such an inquiry can proceed by determining the non-liberal arts enrollments in the states' community colleges and then tracking transfers to the major receiving institutions.

Four messages can be gleaned from the Total Community College Curriculum Study. First, the liberal arts are far from eclipsed in the community college. The decline in liberal arts enrollments through the early 1970s appears to have been halted. Although transfer rates have declined and the cognitive complexity associated with liberal arts study has diminished during the same period (Cohen and Brawer, 1987; Grubb, 1991; Lombardi, 1979; Palmer and Eaton, 1991; Richardson, Fisk, and Okun, 1983), a significant curricular foundation on which to expand the collegiate function does exist. Second, occupational education has not taken over the community college. Claims such as those made by the AACJC (American Association of Community and Junior Colleges, 1986), which maintain that occupational enrollments constitute the majority of enrollments nationally or that the majority of students are enrolled in such programs, are inconsistent with this study's findings.

Third, and of crucial importance to a dominant collegiate function, there is a core of transferable career education curricula in the community college. While the study looks at only five states and, in some cases, at only a few institutions within these states, it does confirm that non-liberal arts coursework is routinely transferable. This transfer may be idiosyncratic, but it does exist.

Fourth, the study is important because it points to other significant questions about the community college curriculum that need to be answered to determine the viability of the collegiate function. The Total Community College Curriculum Study only sorts the labels attached to courses—the traditional credit-bearing vehicles of the community college. As such, it confirms that the first condition of a collegiate community college—that the majority of its offerings be in the liberal arts and career education—is met on a national scale. This sorting, though quite important, does not tell us about what is actually being taught and the level of complexity of these courses. Whether or not the collegiate function has a dominant presence cannot be determined only by confirming the first of the four conditions identified with the collegiate community college. What is taught and whether the instruction is demanding are critical as well. Studies of the classroom experience that examines both content and academic standards need to be undertaken, but the framework of course offerings and enrollments is intact.

Presidents and the Collegiate Function

Another condition for a dominant collegiate function, a campus environment that supports long-term educational goals beyond the associate level for students, requires significant presidential involvement. In December 1991, the National Center for Academic Achievement and Transfer of the American Council on Education, in cooperation with the CSCC, conducted a national random survey of presidents of AACC-affiliated two-year colleges to determine attitudes toward the curriculum (Eaton, 1992c). Of the 218 presidents surveyed, 114, or 53 percent, responded. On average, these chief executive officers were 53 years old and male (88.6 percent) and held graduate degrees in education rather than in academic disciplines. This description of the characteristics of the average president is consistent with earlier studies of the higher education presidency that have included community colleges (Green, 1986). The presidents held their jobs for an average of nine years.

The presidents were asked about the major functions of

the comprehensive community college as expressed through curricular offerings: the collegiate and transfer function (liberal arts), the occupational function (vocational, business, and technological education), the remedial and developmental function, and the community service function (continuing education for personal or professional development). They were also asked about curricular change, including the way course and program approval or deletion took place on their campuses, and were asked to identify trends in community college curricula over the next five years, both nationally and in their institutions. Finally, they were asked to comment on the ways in which their community colleges could be most useful to their respective communities.

The presidents described the curricula of their respective institutions by identifying the distribution of course offerings: the percentage of the curriculum devoted to the liberal arts, occupational education, remedial and developmental education, and community service. They were asked to describe these distributions both at the time they arrived at the institution and at the time of the survey. They also were asked to indicate the distributions they thought were most appropriate — if they had complete freedom of choice in curricular decisions (see Table 4.5).

From this survey it can be seen that presidents do not perceive that there is a single dominant curriculum in their institutions. Offerings are fairly evenly divided between liberal arts and occupational education, with some edge to the liberal arts. Taken together, the liberal arts and occupational education accounted for more than 82 percent of the institution's curricula when the presidents arrived and would, if left to them, decline to 77.3 percent. Growth would occur mainly in the community service curricula. Taken together, community service and remedial and developmental curricula would (if these presidents had their way) grow from 17.0 percent to 22.7 percent, and no single curriculum would be dominant.

The presidents offered two comments on the liberal arts at their respective institutions: it is virtually unchanged in scope since they took office and they would prefer that its scope be modestly reduced. Occupational offerings had declined slightly during the tenure of the presidents and were expected to decline

Table 4.5.

	Liberal Arts	Occupational	Remedial/ Developmental	Community Service	Total
1. What was the percentage of curriculum devoted to these college functions when you *first became* president?	43.17	39.73	9.93	7.17	100
2. What percentages apply *currently*?	42.39	35.89	13.57	8.15	100
3. What are the percentage trends you foresee in the *next five years*?	41.56	34.31	15.32	8.90	100
4. If you had complete choice in the matter, what emphasis would you assign to each of these four functions?	40.67	36.67	11.85	10.81	100

Source: Center for the Study of Community Colleges and the National Center for Academic Achievement and Transfer, American Council on Education, Presidential Leadership and Community College Curricula Study, 1991.

further. The presidents felt that this was appropriate. Remedial and developmental curricula increased during the presidents' time at their institutions, and they expected an additional increase over the next five years. If it were left to them, the presidents would resist this expansion. Community service curricula had been expanding and were expected to expand further in the future. This was viewed by the presidents as desirable.

The presidents were also asked to describe their involvement in curricular change in their institutions. More than two-thirds of them indicated that they had very limited involvement in adoption of new courses or course revision. More than 90 percent reported that they were very much involved in approval of new programs and almost 80 percent reported being very much involved in course or program deletion (see Table 4.6).

Table 4.6.

	Very Much Involved	Involved Very Little
1. New course adoption	30.6	69.4
2. Revised course adoption	15.5	84.5
3. New program approval	92.8	7.2
4. Course or program deletion	79.3	20.5

Source: Center for the Study of Community Colleges and the National Center for Academic Achievement and Transfer, American Council on Education, Presidential Leadership and Community College Curricula Study, 1991.

When asked about national trends they expected to see in the next five years, the presidents anticipated an increased need for remedial education and English as a Second Language programs, followed by an increased demand for curricula to meet transfer needs and a need for additional occupational programs. An increase in community service functions and a decrease in occupational programs were cited as the least likely trends to occur. These predictions would apply to their respective institutions as well (see Table 4.7).

When they were asked how community colleges could be most useful to their communities, the presidents identified, in

Table 4.7.

What trends do you anticipate in the next five years? Please rank order, with 1 indicating the most likely and 5 the least.

	Nationally	At Your College
1. The community college will move toward developing more occupational programs.	2.81	2.8
2. Occupational programs will shrink to meet a diminished variety of fields.	4.04	3.8
3. The number of students transfering will increase.	2.2	2.1
4. The need for English as a Second Language and remedial education will grow to reflect changing populations.	2.1	2.5
5. Community service functions will continue to grow.	3.4	3.3

Source: Center for the Study of Community Colleges and the National Center for Academic Achievement and Transfer, American Council on Education, Presidential Leadership and Community College Curricula Study, 1991.

order of importance, training for future work or upgrading careers, preparing more students for transfer, and stressing developmental and remedial education. Adding student services for personal development, embedding the liberal arts in noncredit instruction, and working to strengthen accreditation were considered least important. This perception of usefulness at the local level was mirrored at the national level (see Table 4.8).

Three major points may be inferred from this survey. First, college presidents have experienced—and expect—little change in the way curricular offerings are distributed at their respective institutions. At the same time, they do expect some changes in both the local and national need for community college services. This can produce discontinuity between curricular offerings and the needs presidents claim their colleges will serve. For example, presidents see occupational education as one of the most useful areas, but they do not anticipate more occupational education offerings. The presidents are more consistent in their opinions on developmental and remedial education, anticipating both a need and an expansion of offerings.

Second, according to the survey, the presidents have lim-

Table 4.8.

How do you think community colleges could be most useful to their communities? Please rank 1, 2, and 3 for the top three and 8 for the bottom statement.

	Nationally	At Your College
1. Train more people for future work or career upgrading.	87.7	91.2
2. Prepare more students for transfer to four-year colleges and universities.	70.2	75.4
3. Stress remedial and developmental education.	62.3	57.0
4. Encourage people to use the community college as a center for their own personal development.	25.4	34.2
5. Embed the liberal arts in noncredit programs in order to expose a greater number of people to the arts and sciences.	4.4	4.4
6. Provide more student services to support academic goals.	15.8	19.3
7. Work directly with four-year institutions to develop productive accreditation policies.	6.8	7.0
8. Establish more student services for personal development.	2.6	1.8
9. Devote more financial resources to complexes for the arts.	0	0

Note: The percentage indicates those who rated usefulness as 1, 2, or 3.
Source: Center for the Study of Community Colleges and the National Center for Academic Achievement and Transfer, American Council on Education, Presidential Leadership and Community College Curricula Study, 1991.

ited involvement in the development of courses—the fundamental building blocks of curricular change—both politically and intellectually. The majority are not highly visible at the early stages of the curricular change process. The development of new programs is sometimes the culmination of a series of independent decisions to adopt individual courses, decisions that have strong implications for what happens at the program level. To remain distant from curricular change at the grass-roots level is to limit a key opportunity to influence the curriculum.

Third, and most important, the presidents in this survey are not yet committed to a dominant collegiate function. Their unwillingness to expand both occupational offerings and liberal arts and transfer offerings confirm this point; it may mean that the presidents are trying to honor their commitment to comprehensiveness through greater balance among offerings at their institutions. Alternatively, it may mean that they want to strengthen their community service and developmental and remedial commitments, seeing, in spite of their views of future trends, that these commitments are important defining elements for their colleges.

Presidents, the Collegiate Commitment, and the Intellectual Life of the College

The president has primary responsibility for the intellectual life of the college — an amalgam of the academic values held by faculty and administrators, the extent to which they engage each other in intellectual inquiry, and their sense of intellectual commitment to their students. The nature and intensity of an institution's intellectual life can be observed through the informal exchanges of professional educators on the campus and the way faculty and administrators handle more formal academic tasks such as curriculum development or making decisions about academic standards. It can also be observed in the number and frequency of opportunities that faculty, administrators, and students develop to engage one another on important academic matters, whether by bringing in outside speakers, developing campus newsletters, or participating in other forms of commentary.

If, as discussed in Chapter Six, a dominant collegiate function enriches the intellectual life of the college, then a president, by helping to build this function, can carry out, at least in part, an important intellectual responsibility for the institution. Presidential impact should be felt through attention to teaching and learning as well as through articulation of the president's academic values. It should be reflected in the extent of his or her participation in formal decision making about the curriculum and other matters of academic policy, and it should be the result of overt efforts to build serious intellectual conversations focused on the collegiate role.

Every president has difficult choices to make about how to make the best use of his or her time and energy. The presidential role requires a considerable commitment to external activities such as working with legislators, public officials, community groups, members of the corporate community, and members of the governing board. Internally, presidents worry about facilities, parking, lawsuits, utility bills, and the budget. All of this — and more — leaves the president with limited time to engage in the academic sphere; as a result, most institutions employ chief academic officers who have the primary responsibility for this area.

Leadership in achieving a dominant collegiate function calls for presidents to rearrange priorities related to the use of their time. They need to either reduce their personal involvement in other spheres of activity, increase their involvement in academic decision making by working with faculty and academic administrators, or both. Priority should be given to curricular considerations with the intent of expanding college-level studies in the liberal arts and career education. Presidents also need to be involved in discussions of academic standards that focus on ensuring college-level expectations of student performance. Their involvement in the intellectual life of the college should concentrate on building the values in the campus environment that are the most conducive to students' reaching long-range educational goals.

Although academic administrators and faculty play key roles here, presidents can also participate in curricular decision making in ways that do not compromise these roles. Although faculty and departments develop courses and programs, presidents should be involved, from time to time, in discussions about the future direction of the various academic areas of the institution. They can take the initiative and begin dialogues throughout the institution on key curricular issues, attend departmental meetings devoted to curricular matters as well as meetings of program advisory committees, and remain active in academic senates and committees that focus on curricular and other academic matters. Contrary to the results of the presidential survey, presidents should be part of the course approval process, raising questions about how course changes affect programs and about the future academic direction of various areas.

Similarly, presidents can address academic standards by working with the faculty and administrators who, from time to time, are called upon to review grading practices and institutional requirements, such as prerequisites and placement testing. If an institution has not raised basic questions about academic standards for a considerable period of time, the president should take the initiative, perhaps establishing a college-wide committee to review these issues. Academic standards and their impact on different students within an institution can be investigated as a basis for determining those students for whom the institution is doing the best job in ensuring student success and those for whom it is doing the least. This can lead to important changes in academic support.

Presidents can hold regular conversations with faculty and administrators and routinely invite knowledgeable speakers to the college to share in these conversations. These sessions can be devoted to fundamental issues of educational importance to the community college, higher education, and the nation. They can provide a foundation for visionary thinking about the future in the areas of teaching and learning, general education, quality in higher education, and multiculturalism, to name only a few topics. Such conversations can become central to the institution's thinking about its effectiveness and its values. Presidents should also teach at least once a year.

If the community college seeks to establish itself as a serious academic institution, the president must *make* the time to stay involved in the academic life of the institution. The president does some of everyone's job, but there are certain tasks within the institution that are uniquely presidential. Providing direction for the intellectual life of the college, articulating that direction, and building investment in it are all responsibilities that rest — first and foremost — with the president.

Summary

The 1991 surveys of curricula and presidential leadership indicate that there were few changes in curricula during the 1980s. The first piece of good news is that the preponderance of transferable liberal arts and non-liberal arts offerings in the community college provide a sound curricular foundation for a dominant collegiate function. The second piece of good news is that presidents *are* involved in curricular decision making. The surveys highlight two major challenges, however. Presidents need to broaden and deepen their involvement in curricular decision making and they need to examine more carefully the extent to which their views of the curriculum fit with local and national needs. The bad news of the survey is that it reflects little presidential commitment to a dominant collegiate function. Presidents can make this commitment, however, and use it to provide leadership in both the curriculum and the intellectual life of the college.

Chapter Five

The Case Against
the Collegiate Community College

This chapter explores the major arguments against a collegiate community college. Although these arguments run counter to the purpose and intent of this book, they are important to an understanding of the range of thinking about the role of the community college. They also provide some warnings about mistakes that can be made when establishing a dominant collegiate function.

The chapter also examines two kinds of actions that might be taken by those who are convinced of the arguments against a dominant collegiate function and want to see it reduced in scope: limiting the collegiate function or eliminating it entirely from the community college mission. It then argues that a third alternative is most likely: an emerging specialization among community colleges where some remain comprehensive institutions, others focus primarily on terminal vocational education, and yet others assume a social service role. The net effect of this type of specialization would be to diminish the collegiate function — and the arguments against the collegiate community college will have carried the day.

Arguments Against a Dominant Collegiate Role

The arguments that are put forward against a strong collegiate role generally include two major points: (1) a strong collegiate function conflicts with the access mission of the community college and (2) the community college could not sustain an effective collegiate function even if it wanted to. The first point is usually made by community college educators who strongly value either the community-based or occupational visions of the community college; the second is usually made by university researchers who focus on the limited educational and economic attainment the community college experience provides for students.

Community college educators arguing for the first point maintain that strengthening the collegiate function will produce negative consequences for community college access. Students in community colleges have a limited ability to successfully undertake collegiate work; this is the avenue pursued by Parnell in his discussion of the "ordinary" student. These educators also argue that the unique institutional place of the community college requires the collegiate function to play a subordinate role and community colleges to be placed outside of the mainstream of higher education; this is Gleazer's position. Cross follows the line of reasoning that the collegiate function is less important than the other purposes of the community college. These thinkers do not argue for elimination of the collegiate function, but for its containment. They want collegiate work, but in an institutional climate in which the other community college functions, such as occupational education and community-based education, are more important.

Those who maintain that the community college is ineffective as a collegiate institution believe that it should leave this work to others. They cite several reasons for collegiate ineffectiveness. Some maintain that student attendance patterns work against a successful collegiate function: the use of the community college as a stop-in and stop-out, part-time, nondegree educational site does not contribute to collegiate effectiveness (Adelman, 1992; Astin, 1982). Others argue against the desirability of the function itself, maintaining that the community colleges *can* do collegiate work, but perform other functions better (Alfred and Linder, 1990; Breneman and Nelson, 1981; Clowes and Levin, 1989). Still others contend that the collegiate function has not produced its desired results and that the community college is structurally ill-suited to carry out the collegiate role (Jencks and Riesman, 1968). The community college leadership, intentionally or unintentionally, is committed to social inequality and will not work to diminish this inequality through emphasizing educational mobility, which, in turn, requires a strong collegiate function. This, as has been discussed, is the approach of Karabel, Pincus, Dougherty, Grubb, and Zwerling (see Chapter Three).

The Mission Arguments

Parnell's strongest argument against the collegiate function is based on his contention that since the majority of American people do not hold the baccalaureate degree, collegiate education should not be the primary focus of the community college. The "ordinary" student, according to Parnell, is not a baccalaureate student. As noted in Chapter Three, Parnell decries the tendency to identify educational excellence, respect, and dignity only with the baccalaureate and to consider education at the subbaccalaureate level as second-rate. Pointing to the range of abilities among students, he rejects the use of a single standard of excellence in an educational setting; he considers the baccalaureate to be used in this way. Parnell believes that educational excellence can be achieved in many ways. Crucial to the discussion here, he believes that rejecting a single standard of excellence means rejecting the collegiate function. If the baccalaureate were one of many standards of excellence, if there were an alternative single standard, or if that single standard were more inclusive — for example, if the associate degree were to be used — it is not clear that the collegiate function would be unacceptable to him even though the same argument applies: the vast majority of community college students do not obtain the associate degree, rendering it, for this population, elitist.

Although Parnell acknowledges the importance of both the comprehensive community college and the collegiate function, he also points to the collegiate function's limitations: "Are we creating the crisis of the 1990's by indiscriminately imposing baccalaureate-degree program standards upon high school graduation requirements? . . . When seventy-five percent or

more of our high-school graduates do not complete the baccalaureate and twenty-five percent of those who begin high school
do not even finish, one must question the validity of the current educational program" (1985b, p. 16). He refers to the well-
established college prep/baccalaureate-degree curriculum when
used as the only definition of educational excellence as one of
the "enemies of excellence" (Parnell, 1990).

Although Parnell's influence is strong, his move to refocus
the community college's mission rests on two assumptions that
cannot be sustained. The first assumption is that baccalaureate
attainment is overvalued in this society and emphasis on this
goal tends to push the community college in the direction of
a single standard of excellence. The second is that the two uni-
verses of ordinary students and baccalaureate recipients are
mutually exclusive. Baccalaureate-degree attainment, if it is
measured by earnings and status, *is* more highly valued than
associate-degree education. Parnell himself (1991) points out,
for example, that the average monthly earnings of baccalaureate-
degree recipients in 1987 were $1,829, while the average associate-
degree recipient earned $1,458. But greater earnings do not
mean that achieving the baccalaureate is the only measure of
excellence in the community college. Nor does it mean that the
baccalaureate is overvalued. Parnell confuses prestige and influence with the existence of a single standard.

With regard to the second assumption, ordinary students
do obtain the baccalaureate in significant numbers. Data from
the 1986 follow-up of *High School and Beyond* (National Center
for Education Statistics, 1991), for example, demonstrate that
41 percent of students in the second and third quartiles of tested
ability obtained the baccalaureate in six years. These are "ordinary" students. Fifty-two percent did not graduate within six
years (Ross, L., personal communication, February 20, 1992),
but this does not mean that they will never graduate. The 41
percent who graduated within six years represent a substantial
graduation rate for middle-level students and certainly are a far
cry from the notion that interest in the baccalaureate should be
confined to an elite.

Gleazer is less direct. By arguing for the community college as a community-based learning site, he is arguing against the traditional notion of the collegiate function of the community college. He believes that the community college's mission is to meet needs that other educational institutions will not or cannot meet. For example, in anticipating the place of community colleges in the 1980s, Gleazer maintains: "In the closing years of the 1970s, community colleges experience a 'novelty of conditions.' . . . The institution which sought a campus and other paraphernalia of the collegiate ways often functions throughout its district and chafes frequently in its collegiate harness even to the point of declaring that the collegiate mode might be defeating its purpose" (Gleazer, 1979, p. 4).

Gleazer (1968) clearly maintains that the collegiate function is not the chief assignment of the community college. He claims that exclusive emphasis on the collegiate function— especially its transfer role—will prevent the community college from addressing the broad range of students, with different abilities and interests, that it has attracted. He says, "To offer only courses preparatory to other courses possibly to be taken at some dim future date is a fraud, even if accompanied by the best of intentions" (p. 52), and he argues that community colleges focus on the connection with higher education because of their reluctance to identify with secondary education and their perception of the prestige of higher education.

Gleazer points out that although two-thirds of the students in community colleges will not transfer, community college programs and procedures are chosen on the assumption that most students will. For this two-thirds of the student population, educational experiences other than those leading to the baccalaureate are essential. The difficulty here rests in part on the difference between what students say they want and what they actually do. Gleazer contends that even though most students will not transfer, two-thirds of them indicate an intent to transfer when they enroll in the community college. This tension between what students say they want and what they do has, according to Gleazer, contributed to the community college's tendency to identify with traditional higher education.

Cross (1990) argues that community colleges were created

to "break the mold" of traditional higher education. She perceives a "rush to make transfer the priority mission of the community college" and maintains that this will reduce educational opportunity and will not serve the majority of students well. Cross wants community colleges to continue to break the mold and believes that an emphasis on transfer — an example of the community college's preoccupation with traditional higher education — betrays the commitment that was made when junior colleges became comprehensive community colleges. She claims that few students who enter the community college want the baccalaureate and argues that a strong transfer function is being used as a single standard of excellence that is inappropriate. Cross offers a number of suggestions, including strengthening occupational education and building better connections between occupational and liberal arts programs, to satisfy her concern about overemphasis on the collegiate function.

The Effectiveness Arguments

The tone for arguments about the effectiveness of the collegiate function was set by Jencks and Riesman (1968), just as community college enrollments were growing at a rapid rate. Jencks and Riesman question whether these two-year institutions should even be called colleges. They describe community colleges as institutions that "show comparatively little deference to professional academic opinion about how an institution of higher learning should be run, and consequently teach both subjects and students whom most scholars regard as worthless" (p. 480). They are not "real" colleges or effective collegiate institutions. Jencks and Riesman maintain that the students in community colleges are marginal, that community colleges are a site of popular rather than academic culture, and that their governing boards do not have an educational vision derived from personal experience with academic culture. They argue that their faculty do not sustain traditional discipline-based education and that there is little room for innovation. Like the students, the faculty are academically marginal. As transfer institutions, community colleges are not in control of their academic destiny, but must rely on the direction of senior institutions. This prevents the community college from emerging as a site of academic creativity and resourcefulness.

In discussing the impact of the community college, Jencks and Riesman point out that, according to the available data, the community college is not a viable route to the baccalaureate. They also challenge the perception that the community college is low-cost, noting the lack of clear evidence that the cost per student in the community college is any less than the cost per lower-division student in a senior institution and contending that the community college attracts students who are academically marginal and who would not otherwise have gone to college. The college attendance of academically marginal students actually increases taxpayer expense.

In a somewhat similar vein, thirteen years later, Breneman and Nelson make a powerful statement against the collegiate function of the community college: "We favor an educational division of labor among institutions in the 1980s that would result in the community colleges enrolling fewer full-time academic transfer students of traditional college age and retaining a dominant position in those activities that four-year institutions have not undertaken traditionally and are likely to do less well" (Breneman and Nelson, 1981, p. 211f). Using information collected from various national studies, state investigations, and campus visits, the authors conclude that the traditional academic transfer function of the community college — the collegiate function — is its least successful undertaking.

Breneman and Nelson contend, first, that community colleges are not primarily transfer institutions. They examined state- and institution-specific studies contained in fifty-one reports covering nineteen states, and the only consistent finding that emerged was that few community college students graduate or transfer to a four-year institution. At the national level, studies confirm that attending a community college rather than a four-year school tends to reduce the probability that a student will earn the baccalaureate within 4½ years after high school graduation. Choosing a community college has a negative effect on the amount of education received during the first few years after high school.

Second, Breneman and Nelson maintain that community colleges experience more confusion about their mission than any other sector of higher education or even elementary and secondary education. The differences in governance, financing, and programs in community colleges in various parts of the country have produced a lack of consensus about this mission at the daily operating level, in spite of the apparent consensus in community college literature about a comprehensive mission. These differences have widespread implications for obtaining state support to fund community colleges and for building public policy support generally; they make it difficult for community colleges to sustain a public education campaign that represents them as viable collegiate institutions.

Third, Breneman and Nelson point out that while community colleges have a comparative advantage over four-year colleges and universities in vocational-technical education, remedial education, and noncredit community services, they do not have an advantage over four-year colleges and universities in traditional undergraduate education. Among other factors, the local orientation of the community college weakens its strategic position in offering traditional undergraduate education. A local orientation works well for placebound adults; it is inadequate for students, for whom experiences beyond the local community are especially valuable. Breneman and Nelson believe that community colleges may best serve the public and themselves by sticking to what they do best.

Breneman and Nelson leave the community colleges with three strategies to ponder: (1) making a commitment to a comprehensive mission, (2) dropping their strong community service orientation, and (3) placing renewed emphasis on traditional collegiate functions—a "back to basics" strategy in which these institutions become community-based learning centers. Their research strongly suggests that none of these strategies will be successful, however, and that the community college needs to find an alternative role that is not collegiate but that the public values—and is willing to fund. This alternate role would deemphasize the academic transfer function and encourage the other community college functions such as vocational education, developmental and remedial education, and community service. Nunley's additional analysis of traditional students who pursue the baccalaureate by entering the community college after high school confirms Breneman and Nelson's original findings and the difficulty they pose for community college decision makers (Eaton, 1988).

Astin (1982, 1983) has consistently argued that community colleges cannot be successful collegiate institutions because baccalaureate-degree attainment is less likely for those who begin their educational career in a community college rather than a four-year institution. He cites the lack of residential facilities, low student involvement in the life of the college, and the obstacles imposed by the very act of moving from one institution to another. He also argues that the presence of the community college may have the effect of *reducing* educational opportunity: community colleges may attract students who would otherwise have enrolled in a four-year institution, thereby reducing the likelihood that they will persist to the point of obtaining the baccalaureate degree.

Reviewing data on 1972 high school graduates who attended the community college, Astin (1982) also points out that many students who begin collegiate education in a community college want to obtain the baccalaureate degree. He recommends that community colleges revitalize their transfer function through a programmatic approach to creating a community for transfer students that would include the intensive educational experiences and extracurricular activities of residential four-year schools. He also urges community colleges to work closely with senior institutions, provide remediation programs for potential transfer students, and identify funds to meet their financial aid needs. He has limited confidence in these efforts, however, and further recommends that if students seeking the baccalaureate are located in an area where they have a choice between a community college and a senior institution, they should attend the latter. For the past twenty-five years, Astin has consistently affirmed both the limited capacity of the community college to provide a viable collegiate function and the desire of many who attend to undertake collegiate studies and transfer.

Alfred questions the value of the collegiate function because it interferes with his primary criterion for general community college effectiveness: responsiveness to community needs. While his definition of effectiveness is complex, its essential point is "the capacity of community colleges to help individuals and groups to adapt to changing conditions and needs" (Alfred and Linder, 1990, p. 3). The community college is effective if it is responsive. Alfred's model of effectiveness is in the tradition of the Gleazer community-based vision of the community college, and his statement of institutional purpose is similarly vague. Because he does not want to stipulate parameters for responsiveness, he would resist the idea of the dominance of any one function of the community college, including the collegiate function. Community colleges must maintain flexibility. Effectiveness, he argues, "is determined by the presence of paradox. . . . Paradox exists when community colleges employ what seem to be contradictory yet equally necessary programs. . . . to adapt to rapidly changing conditions and needs in the service region. . . . *No choice need be made between them*" (my italics) (p. 2).

Alfred also stresses that the responsiveness of the community college can be controlled through successful negotiation by the community college with its community. The community college, according to Alfred, is not totally demand-driven. Instead, it is a successful negotiator in a semipolitical environment. This means that community demand is shaped and influenced through the political authority of the community college, which becomes a "power institution." The basis for this power is threefold, consisting of the community's comfort with the college, the local focus of the college, and the perception that the community college is a "safe" institution (Alfred, personal communication, July 17, 1992; Alfred, Peterson, and White, 1992).

Alfred has a view of the liberal arts that does not require the community college to sustain a primary emphasis on the collegiate function; in his vision of the effective community college, discipline based on interdisciplinary education is not intrinsically valued and a major emphasis on transfer is absent. Instead he calls for an emphasis on technical education, with liberal arts education secondary. The liberal arts are of value for developing critical thinking and other transferable skills. In an earlier discussion of the need for flexibility throughout the organization, Alfred (Eaton, 1988) talks about improving college and university partnerships by sharing facilities, research on teaching and learning effectiveness, strategic planning information, and systems technology. He does not envision the relationship between two-year and four-year institutions as academic in nature and shows little concern about faculty, the curriculum, or academic expectations.

Adelman (personal communication, January 28, 1992) argues that the way students use the community college renders it ineffective as a collegiate institution. He describes the community college as an "occasional" educational institution: students take few courses and attend intermittently. They are not following prescribed educational programs, have little sustained contact with faculty, and do not pursue degrees. This creates a community college culture in which almost no goals for educational attainment have been established. For Adelman, a focus on goals is essential to a successful collegiate function. Community colleges, he states, are really secondary schools. They lack the emphasis on persistence, the structure, the concern for learning development, and the goal orientation that is considered essential for a collegiate institution. Four-year schools—even urban-based, predominantly commuter institutions—possess these features. In his study of the 1972 high school graduates who attended community colleges (1992), Adelman maintains that the institution accommodates student decisions "to engage in learning on their own terms, and in their own time." Students use the community college for ad hoc purposes; credentialing appears to be of limited significance.

For Clowes and Levin (1989), when the community college continues to pursue the collegiate function, it contributes to confusion and a lack of consensus about its mission, what they call "mission drift." Clowes and Levin explore the notion of a needed "core function" for the community college that can provide identity and justification for its existence. They contend that academic transfer education will not be the core function of the future because, according to the available data, the competition between community colleges and nonselective four-year institutions has resulted in the latter becoming the primary providers of collegiate and academic transfer education. Clowes and Levin view remedial education and community service as marginal rather than core functions for an institution of higher education. They conclude that the only viable core function for the community college is career education. They do not maintain that the community college cannot handle the collegiate function; instead, they point out that the community colleges and four-year nonselective institutions have been competitors in the lower-division liberal arts arena and the four-year schools have prevailed. Other circumstances, including diminished enrollments in the liberal arts, the emphasis on career education, and the drift in the community college's mission, have contributed to this as well. Sustaining the collegiate function would produce harm by diverting the community college from building career education as its core function.

Some university-based critics of the community college maintain that it is not an effective collegiate institution because, if it were, it would promote educational mobility for greater numbers of students. Their arguments were noted earlier in this chapter. Studies of educational attainment in the community college to date tend to confirm their criticisms. These studies show that attendance at a community college is less likely to lead to baccalaureate-degree acquisition than attendance at a four-year institution and that occupational education in the community college does not clearly result in social or economic gains that would not have been realized without the community college experience (Pascarella and Terenzini, 1991).

Accepting the Arguments: Diminishing Collegiate Emphasis

For those who are persuaded by the arguments that the collegiate role should not be the dominant function of the community college, several alternatives remain. First, a collegiate role can be retained but continue to function only as a limited part of the comprehensive mission of the community college. Second, the collegiate role can be completely eliminated from the community college mission. And third, community college educators can give up any expectation that the national community college enterprise will share a single vision or common mission and acknowledge that community colleges will undergo a period of institutional specialization that may — or may not — include the collegiate function. The impact of each of these alternatives will be to diminish the collegiate function.

Retaining a Limited Collegiate Role

As was discussed earlier, many community college educators resist the collegiate function as the principal role of the community college, but few would eliminate it entirely. One possible alternative is to limit the collegiate role. This can be done by making it terminal or subjugating it to the needs of occupational education.

With a limited collegiate function, the community college's transfer role would be retained while its importance in relation to other functions would be greatly diminished. The collegiate function would, instead, serve a terminal general education function. This would mean that the liberal arts offerings would provide general skill development. These offerings would probably not be transferable. A collegiate function that is subordinate to occupational education would serve occupational education by determining the curricular content of liberal arts offerings according to the needs of the occupational area and not the liberal arts discipline itself. Courses such as anatomy and physiology in nursing programs, physics in engineering programs, and English in business programs would cease to function as introductions to a discipline and become a survey of principles or concepts of importance to the occupational area they serve.

Limiting the collegiate role would mean that the community college would reduce its ties to the broader higher education enterprise. Students who tried to transfer would have had a more restricted collegiate experience than native students. The limited collegiate emphasis in their coursework and the values of the community college environment might not have adequately prepared them for the four-year environment. Faculty in the community college would continue to be distanced from any national intellectual community, and public support for community colleges that depended on a more expansive collegiate role would be eroded.

On the other hand, the community college would be free to develop its institutional agenda unencumbered by major concerns about the rest of the higher education enterprise such as conditions for transferability of courses or acceptance of the associate degree by four-year institutions. Access would be enhanced because college-level skills would not be essential for many courses. The community college would have greater freedom to experiment with new general education curricula and could focus additional attention on both occupational and community-based efforts.

Eliminating the Collegiate Function

Community colleges, it can be argued, do not need a collegiate function. Collegiate education is available elsewhere and may inhibit the community college as it attempts to satisfy its roles relating to access and community development. If, as much of the data indicate, the collegiate function is not effective in the community college, it does not need to be offered; students who wish to pursue the baccalaureate can go directly to a four-year institution. The community college could be entirely devoted to the "middle" students of whom Parnell speaks (1985b). Responsiveness would not be hampered by having to acquiesce to at least some of the norms and values of the traditional collegiate world.

Eliminating the collegiate function would have a number of effects on two-year institutions. First, all community colleges would become either technical colleges or community education centers. Second, community colleges would no longer be part of higher education. They would function as sites of terminal education and would probably become similar in many ways to two-year private career schools. Third, community colleges would become smaller as their liberal arts faculty and administrators were phased out. Fourth, community colleges would no longer need to be concerned with educational mobility beyond the associate-degree level. The community college critics who base their negative assessment of the community college on its failure to lead to the baccalaureate degree would become irrelevant. Fifth, community colleges would become more costly on a per capita basis. Because providing the collegiate function costs comparatively less than providing career or remedial education, the average cost per student would increase for the taxpayer.

Serious public policy implications are associated with eliminating the collegiate function in the community college. It would force four-year colleges and universities to reconsider access and pay additional attention to mass education. They would be pressured to admit more students who do not meet their current criteria of academic preparedness and would have to focus more attention on undergraduate education, especially lower-division work. The elimination of the collegiate function in the community college would create a de facto tracking system at the upper levels of education. Those who attended a community college with no collegiate function would effectively be tracked into lower-paying, lower-status jobs than those who attended four-year institutions. This tracking system could exacerbate the existing problem of differences in educational and economic attainment among different racial groups. The community college with a collegiate function is an important entry point to higher education, especially for black and Hispanic students. If minority groups cannot attend a four-year institution instead of a community college, then the de facto tracking system will be described — accurately — as racist.

Allowing Institutional Specialization

If they are left alone, it is unlikely that community colleges will significantly limit or entirely eliminate the collegiate function from their operations. What is likely is an emerging specialization of function *within* the community college enterprise. This specialization would be unplanned and unanticipated and could be the result of what some have called "mission drift" (Clowes and Levin, 1989; Cross, 1981). It would result in three major kinds of two-year institutions, only one of which would sustain the collegiate function. Institutions that are presently designated as community colleges would be either comprehensive two-year colleges that include a transfer component, technical institutes, or social service centers (Eaton, 1990). The major impact of this specialization would be a diminution of access to collegiate education throughout the country. Three factors already familiar to community college educators could produce this specialization: (1) the community college's commitment to responsiveness, (2) pressures on the institution to solve social problems that are not primarily educational in nature, and (3) the limited skills that students bring to an open-admission, nonselective institution.

Conditions Favoring Institutional Specialization. Three conditions are critical here. First, the history of the importance of the contemporary responsiveness doctrine within the community college enterprise encourages specialization. This doctrine dates back to the Truman Commission of 1947 and especially to Gleazer and his emphasis on the community college's commitment to community development. This has been a powerful doctrine that has been consistently encouraged by the leadership of the community college and reinforced by the large number of public community colleges that came to dominate the smaller number of private two-year institutions. The responsiveness doctrine has resulted in the community college curriculum becoming an amalgam of courses and services centered around the principle of response to community needs, which has kept the community college from making institutional judgments about what to offer and to whom. In the face of demonstrated community interest in a particular program or service, it is the rare community college leader who will say no on the grounds that, for example, a new degree program or training program does not fit within the current academic priorities of his or her institution.

Second, pressures to solve social problems that are not

primarily educational in nature contribute to specialization. These pressures have created community colleges whose major emphasis is on social services rather than collegiate education. This usually occurs in areas where the community college is serving an economically and social distressed student population, who need services such as child care, financial counseling, homeless shelters, family assistance, and job-seeking assistance that may not be available elsewhere. If social services that should be provided by a city or neighborhood are not available, the community college is the only stable public institution to which the community can turn. This may happen in urban centers as well as in smaller communities that may be suburban or rural as well. Over a long period of time, these social services drive out collegiate work as budgets are reallocated to social services at the expense of traditional instruction and as a college's culture focuses on these services and ceases to invest energy in the initial reason for which it was created.

Third, the limited academic skills that students frequently bring with them when entering the community college can also contribute to specialization. Students' limitations and inability to do college-level work have forced the community college into developmental and remedial studies to an unprecedented extent. Virtually all public two-year colleges offer these courses. State studies in Illinois, Washington, and Kansas show remedial offerings that make up 13 to 16 percent of enrollments (Cohen and Brawer, 1989). In addition, lack of preparedness has affected college-level coursework by causing the amount and level of work required of students to be reduced (Cohen and Brawer, 1987, 1989; Richardson, Fisk, and Okun; 1983). Students read less and less challenging works. They taker fewer essay tests and write fewer papers. Their attendance may be sporadic. The pressure to provide services to underprepared students diverts the budget from college-level programs to developmental and remedial studies, influences the faculty to make fewer college-level demands in the classroom, and reduces the impetus for the faculty to develop college-level programs.

Three Institutional Types. If more movement toward institutional specialization were to take place, the community college with a transfer component would remain as the typical example of the first institutional type, a comprehensive community college. The strength of its collegiate function would vary with the enrollment demands of the community it serves. This would be the least remarkable aspect of specialization.

The second institutional type, the community college turned technical institute, would demonstrate a combination of the community college's commitment to responsiveness and the impact of Parnell's vision of the community college. Any collegiate function would diminish in importance in this type of institution. Concern about economic growth and development, the recession that began in the late 1980s, and international competitiveness, as well as the responsiveness doctrine, would also encourage an emerging technical institute. This trend would be reinforced by the status of the United States as the only developed nation with no formal system of postsecondary vocational training (Thurow, 1992). Public financial support for community colleges is primarily state, not local, and states perceive education's primary responsibility to be to strengthen the economy. They tend to identify the two-year school with technical education and not with the liberal arts or research.

The third institutional type, the community college turned social service center, would result from pressures to solve social problems for which other institutional responses are inadequate. It is already possible to identify institutions that call themselves colleges but do not allocate funds to college-level courses, do not graduate students, and have a negligible transfer function. One public policy issue to be addressed is whether these community colleges should continue to refer to themselves as colleges when they do not have a collegiate function or whether they should formally take on the social service functions to which they have fallen heir and cease to identify themselves as collegiate institutions.

Summary

The arguments against a dominant collegiate function are of two types: those based on the mission of the community college and those based on the effectiveness of the community college as a collegiate institution. Those who use mission to argue against a dominant collegiate function point to the varying needs of the students served by the community college, which go far beyond collegiate education, and to the extent to which access would be compromised, thereby destroying a unique dimension of the community college's role.

Those who use effectiveness to argue against a dominant collegiate function maintain that the community college does not carry out its responsibility to college-level learning as successfully as other educational institutions. They further maintain that the community college manages occupational education, developmental and remedial education, and community services better than its competitors.

If those who oppose a dominant collegiate function prevail, three scenarios might emerge. First, the community college might continue its transfer component, but this function would not rank high in importance compared to others in the community college. This would produce a limited collegiate role. Second, the collegiate function might be eliminated entirely. Third, the national family of community colleges might evolve into a loose community of two-year institutions more remarkable for their differences than their similarities. Three kinds of two-year colleges might be developed: comprehensive community colleges, or those with a modest commitment to a collegiate function; technical institutes, or those with a dominant terminal vocational function; and social service centers, or those with a dominant social service function. This last scenario of institutional specialization is the most likely to occur.

Chapter Six

The Case for
Strengthening Collegiate Education

This chapter describes the collegiate function of the community college and makes a case for its dominance. It examines the implications of a collegiate community college for a commitment to comprehensiveness and reviews the history of controversy that has surrounded the collegiate commitment. It then explores why it is important for the collegiate function to be dominant and how the collegiate community college provides gains for students, society, and the institution itself. The discussion is based on the belief that the community college provides its best and most important service by making the collegiate function dominant.

Describing the Collegiate Function

Four conditions must be present for any community college to sustain a dominant collegiate presence: (1) structured, sequential liberal arts and career education offerings dominate the curriculum; (2) primary attention is given to the development of college-level competencies; (3) the community college environment, through the values it shares with students, ensures, to the greatest extent possible, that students are prepared for baccalaureate study, whether it is pursued immediately after community college attendance or at some later point in a student's educational career; and (4) students can transfer with ease.

A collegiate community college will use course content

similar to that of other lower-division efforts in junior or senior institutions, sustain performance expectations at the level of cognitive complexity that is generally acknowledged as characteristic of lower-division work throughout higher education, and maintain an institutional culture that values, supports, and encourages the collegiate experience. It does this by means such as establishing the collegiate function as primary in planning and institutional statements of purpose, building strong relationships with other higher education institutions, and strongly supporting the faculty who teach collegiate work. *Collegiate* refers to (1) the curricula, or academic content, being taught; (2) the level of instruction; and (3) the institutional context, or environment, in which the curricula are offered. In an ideal setting, the collegiate function influences and informs all other aspects of the institutional mission.

As presented here, the term *college-level* is central to the description of the collegiate role. While there are no precise definitions of it in the literature, community colleges identify college-level work whenever they decide that some courses are designed for transfer while others are developmental or remedial. Four-year schools, similarly, indicate their understanding of what college-level work is when they judge some coursework as transferable from the community college and other coursework as unacceptable. These are acknowledgments that shared understandings exist among institutions about what can be considered collegiate.

The college-level character of the curriculum refers to the intellectual goals set by classroom faculty for the course content and academic tasks that are assigned. These goals have two characteristics: (1) they encompass subject matter that goes beyond the level of high school general education yet precedes the academic specialization characteristic of upper-division and graduate-level university work and (2) they incorporate qualitative and quantitative skill development aimed at ensuring that students can complete baccalaureate liberal arts and career studies if they wish.

College-level work is demanded of students when faculty assign tasks that require creative thinking, the ability to coherently articulate ideas orally and in writing, and the ability to reach and defend conclusions. It is the quality that Richardson, Fisk, and Okun (1983) argue is increasingly missing from the community college — critical literacy. They contrast critical literacy with certain academic tasks such as rote recitation or objective tests, which they call bitting. Bitting is information transfer without analysis, synthesis, or original expression (p. xii). *College-level* is also the phrase Cohen uses to distinguish remedial education from higher learning (Vaughan and Associates, 1983).

College-level academic tasks enable students to develop analytic and synthetic reasoning abilities, to understand and replicate theory, and to function at a conceptual level that reflects creative thought and careful scrutiny of intellectual constructs. History students go beyond quizzes about the "facts" of World War II to analyze the causes and repercussions of the war. English students write essays comparing literary works as well as demonstrating their understanding of the plot of a given novel. Science students can perform experiments and analyze results as well as take objective tests. Students are encouraged to set goals such as achieving the associate or baccalaureate degrees or becoming qualified for employment requiring college-level skills.

This description of college-level study is limited, but the luxury of applying more specific tests to determine college-level work is not available. The higher education community has not been willing to be more precise about defining the division between the collegiate level and other levels of study. What is considered to be college-level study rests on shared understandings that are not described with consistency or precision and that may vary over time.

An institutional culture that supports college-level study will make a public and clear commitment to this role for the community college. In addition to providing support and leadership to faculty engaged in college-level work, it will sustain a comprehensive network of services focused on encouraging students to establish and realize long-range educational goals. It will develop strong ties with other junior and senior institutions at the faculty and administrative levels through teaching exchanges, team teaching, and academic compacts about coursework and programs. Bridge programs such as summer seminars and simultaneous enrollment will be established. College-level study will drive short- and long-range decision making, planning, and budgeting for the institution and will be the primary concern of the president, senior administration, and board of trustees.

College-level study and a dominant collegiate role cannot be effectively sustained in community colleges that do not stress a structured, sequential educational experience that can lead to a degree or other credential or fill distribution or general education requirements. It cannot be effectively maintained in institutions where the majority of institutional investment is in social service work such as child care, work with poverty centers, or drug rehabilitation. And it cannot be sustained if it is overshadowed by developmental and remedial work, occupational studies that are not college-level, or noncredit community service.

Establishing the collegiate commitment of a community college also requires attention to public perception—and this can be frustrating. On one hand, the collegiate role appears obvious. The community college is a citizen of the higher education community; as such, it is expected to carry out the civic duties that are considered important to that community. These duties include study in the discipline-based liberal arts, general education, or interdisciplinary education. They include expectations of college-level intellectual work by students, as well as a community college commitment to working with four-year schools in order to gain formal recognition of two-year coursework or programs.

On the other hand, affirmation of the collegiate role is elusive, because even if community colleges do these things, they are still perceived as less than collegiate. There is much disagreement about whether community college offerings are intellectually equivalent to four-year work and whether career education offerings can be genuinely collegiate. It is also elusive because when community colleges attempt to be intellectually assertive through unique general education or interdisciplinary programs, they find it frustrating — if not impossible — to have these programs accepted by four-year schools.

Despite the apparent similarity in lower-division liberal arts work in two-year and four-year institutions, four-year institutions are sometimes reluctant to sanction community college offerings. There are few states in which, for example, the associate degree is acknowledged as fully equivalent to the first two years of a baccalaureate program. In many states, students complain about their failure to obtain equivalent credit in course-for-course transfer and about being forced to accept general or elective credit for community college coursework. When community colleges create idiosyncratic general education programs, they do so at their own — and their students' — peril: four-year schools resist equivalency credit for these offerings, no matter how high the quality or creative the educational fare.

The Collegiate Function and Comprehensiveness

Many community college educators view the collegiate function as a part of what they term the "comprehensive" community college. They believe that when they support comprehensiveness, they are routinely supporting the collegiate function. Comprehensiveness refers to the community college's commitment to four purposes: liberal arts and transfer education, occupational education, developmental and remedial education, and community service. In this context, commitment to the collegiate function would not be any more important than occupational education or community-based education. The purposes are valued equally.

But commitment to the collegiate function as part of comprehensiveness is not equivalent to making it dominant. This approach is not assertive enough to establish the collegiate role as central in the community college. Community college educators must go beyond the standard statement about the importance of the collegiate role as one of the several purposes inherent in comprehensiveness and assert clearly and forcefully the enormous importance of this role. The question "How can the community college be most effective in the future?" needs to be answered, "By strengthening the collegiate role so that it functions as a core commitment to college-level studies and provides a context for other community college decision making, values, and activity."

Further, although comprehensiveness is highly regarded in much of the community college literature, it does have some negative effects. First, it is sometimes disparagingly referred to as attempting to be "all things to all people." In this interpretation, a commitment to comprehensiveness by leaders of community colleges suggests that they cannot make up their minds about what is educationally important. Second, when *comprehensiveness* is used in relation to the nationwide collection of community colleges, the term is misleading. It implies a philosophical or ideological unity that, in actuality, is lacking among community colleges, and it masks a failure to make decisions about the special educational role of individual community colleges. Third, comprehensiveness has hampered development of the measures of effectiveness that are needed to demonstrate the value of the community college. It has done this by forcing a broad, loose mission on the community college; community college educators have had limited success developing indicators of effectiveness for the diverse and large array of services that are accommodated under its umbrella. Critics of the community college have taken advantage of this situation: they have aggressively selected among the array to set the terms and conditions that represent the community college's success or failure to the general public; they have become the primary indicators of effectiveness and de facto judges of the community college.

Fourth, at the institutional level, community college educators have allowed themselves to be trapped by their commitment to comprehensiveness. They believe that this commitment prevents them from identifying some purposes as more important than others. Educators at hundreds of institutions write mission statements that include an obligation to comprehensiveness or at least rhetorical commitment to giving equal value to the various purposes of the community college. In reality, institutional leaders, through the decisions they make about investment of resources, constantly indicate that some purposes are more important than others. Moreover, these same leaders consistently and proudly assert that their institutions are highly responsive to local community needs. Some recommend responding to local needs through occupational education; others stress the transfer function. An uncritical use of comprehensiveness at the institutional level becomes an obstacle to choosing between the various purposes to meet local needs.

A dominant collegiate function forces community college leaders to acknowledge that they are making choices about the purposes contained in the community college's mission. In this case, their choice is for the collegiate purpose. A dominant collegiate function lessens the importance of the community college's other purposes and becomes a foundation for them. The shift here is from accepting the four purposes as roughly equal to asserting that one purpose — the collegiate function — is more important than the others. This does not preclude other purposes, but it does subordinate them to the collegiate function. The community college's commitments to developmental and remedial education, occupational education, and community service would have to be honored in the context of its established collegiate commitment.

Controversy About the Collegiate Function

The collegiate role has always been part of community colleges, with the exception of technical institutes or colleges whose charters specifically exclude liberal arts transfer work. At most, these institutes make up 20 percent of the institutions generally considered part of the community college enterprise (Cohen, 1988).

Nonetheless, the collegiate role has always been controversial. In the early junior college years it was controversial because of the perception that the collegiate role was the two-year college's way of appeasing four-year colleges and universities. Junior colleges were accused of either mindlessly replicating the work of senior institutions or imitating them in order to receive sanction within the higher education community. Some impatient junior college leaders felt that there was nothing unique about the collegiate role; they could not argue, as they would have preferred to do, that they were providing a special educational service, in spite of their desire to claim their new institutions as different or special.

During the years in which the emphasis shifted from the junior college to the community college, the collegiate role was controversial because it was traditional. To use Gleazer's phrase (Gleazer, 1980), community colleges were "trapped in tradition." Parnell's orientation toward terminal occupational education and his insistence that baccalaureate education should not be the goal for the majority of community college students rendered the collegiate role suspect. The Truman Commission of 1947, in setting a primarily occupational role for the community college, further challenged the worth of the collegiate role and made primary allegiance to it suspect.

The collegiate role was also controversial in the 1960s and 1970s because it challenged the liberal orthodoxy that supported the community college's strong commitment to vocationalism. Liberals liked the dedication to access of the open-door community college and the vocationalized community college's apparently effective response to the academic limitations of most students who entered through the open-admission process (Brint and Karabel, 1989). The traditional collegiate emphasis called both access and vocationalism into question.

In the 1980s, controversy about the collegiate role extended to minority enrollments. The community college was criticized for doing both too little and too much. It did too little because too few minority students were enrolled in college-level courses, earned the associate degree, and went on to four-year schools. It did too much by emphasizing the collegiate function in the face of evidence that minorities were not benefiting from it. This was interpreted as an exclusionary attitude by community colleges, in which they abandoned their commitment to opportunity through participation.

However ambivalent junior or community college educators are about the collegiate role, few have vigorously sought its elimination from the community college's mission. Many criticize the collegiate role or are threatened by its presence in the two-year college, but no one wishes to do without it. Gleazer and Parnell, along with many others, might wish to downplay this role, but they do not totally ignore it. Ironically, Parnell may have contributed to an expansion of the collegiate role through his emphasis on occupational education—but not in the way he intended. Although he envisioned more occupational education, he saw it primarily as terminal rather than transfer education. The vocationalizing of all of higher education in the 1970s increased the numbers of students in occupational programs. By the 1980s, job requirements escalated as a result of the growth of electronic technology and the changing needs of industry. This produced, for the community college, a situation similar to that of the early years junior college, in which semiprofessional programs led to transfer. In the 1980s, occupational programs were becoming collegiate. The liberal arts still constituted the primary focus of collegiate studies, but programs such as computer science, health-related offerings, and human service career education led to transfer as well as employment and came to be considered collegiate as well.

What Is to Be Gained
from a Dominant Collegiate Function?

Three major gains result from making the collegiate function dominant: (1) gains for students through enhanced educational mobility, (2) gains for society because of the community college's strategic capacity to provide effective collegiate education for nontraditional students, and (3) gains for the two-year college itself through intellectual enrichment.

The perception that educational mobility, nontraditional collegiate education, and intellectual enrichment are gains is, in turn, based on three judgments about what is important for the community college to do. The first judgment is that it is important for these institutions to engage in college-level work rather than precollege study or noncredit work. The second is that it is important for the community college to be part of the higher education enterprise rather than elementary and secondary education or more general civic and cultural educational efforts. The third is that it is important to define the community college's responsibility to access in terms of achievement—especially baccalaureate achievement—rather than only in terms of participation.

The judgment to have community colleges engage in college-level work reflects a traditional view of higher education as a graded, structured experience involving mastery of various levels of intellectual competence that can take place only if a minimum level of cognitive skill is brought to the task. It values levels of scholarship and inquiry that have historically been a part of the collegiate enterprise and is based on the belief that collegiate institutions do not perform the task of elementary and secondary education either efficiently or effectively. This judgment is grounded in the notion that diminution of the quality and scope of academic expectations renders a college other than collegiate.

The second judgment, that community colleges should function within the higher education enterprise, is based on valuing not only the low-cost, convenient, high-quality experience the community college provides for students, but also the additional benefits provided by placing this experience within the higher education framework. For greater advancement of economic, social, and educational attainment and mobility, connecting the two-year institution to the enterprise to which students will go in the future as opposed to the enterprise from which they came provides the proper focus for educational efforts. Being part of higher education allows students to look forward; remaining part of elementary and secondary education cuts off their educational future.

The third judgment, to define access in terms of achievement as well as participation, is intended to provide students with some assurance of educational accomplishment and to take a stand against the notion that a community college serves as an institution that has multiple levels of educational experimentation, no conditions for success, and a sanctioning of failure. The preference for achievement values intelligent and fair discrimination based on demonstrated skill and requires minimum intellectual competencies in order to create an academic environment that produces student learning.

Gain One: Educational and Economic
Attainment and Mobility for Students

Students gain from a dominant collegiate function because it enables them to pursue either the baccalaureate degree, more rewarding employment, or both. It is key to further education. If students are successful, their educational accomplishment is greater and their economic gain and mobility are enhanced. Beyond any economic and occupational gain, this can result in a richer personal life, a greater capacity for civic participation, and a more challenging intellectual life. While there is certainly no need to disparage the educational and economic gains at the associate-degree level, it is also difficult to deny the value of the greater gains that are likely to accrue from a baccalaureate degree and its impact on occupational status and earnings.

Considerable evidence exists to verify the economic advantages of more education. Baccalaureate-degree recipients have higher incomes and status than associate-degree recipients. In 1984, the median income of people with the baccalaureate degree was $22,092; for those with the associate degree, the median income was $16,152 (Carter, 1990). In 1987, the mean monthly income of baccalaureate-degree holders was $2,109; for associate-degree holders, it was $1,609 (American Association of Community and Junior Colleges, 1991). In 1989, the median annual income of workers twenty-five or older with five or more years of college was $32,050. For those with one to three years of college, the median income was $21,631 (National Center for Education Statistics, 1991). Those with more education have more occupational flexibility and access to better jobs. Approximately 53 percent of baccalaureate recipients in 1985–86 held professional, managerial, or technical positions. Between 1970 and 1989, annual income generally rose more rapidly for men with higher levels of educational attainment than those with lower levels (National Center for Education Statistics, 1991). Individuals with lower levels of educational attainment are also more likely to be unemployed. Between 1977 and 1990, income disparity widened most rapidly between college graduates and those who did not graduate from high school (Reich, 1991).

The economics of educational attainment strongly suggests that the road to higher education, for those who begin with the community college, must routinely lead beyond the associate-degree level to additional levels of education. Educational mobility cannot stop with only two full years of college work, as valuable as this may be. Here the community college critics who are concerned about class-based tracking have a point. It is not necessary to agree with their contention that community colleges are *intentionally* reinforcing social inequality to nonetheless realize that they are fulfilling only a minor part of their social and educational responsibility if they fail to move substantial numbers of students from two-year institutions to four-year institutions or more rewarding employment. Access must be defined as a long-term commitment to pursue educational goals beyond the associate-degree level.

The collegiate community college is particularly valuable given the extent to which it serves low-income and first-generation college-going students. In Fall 1989, almost 20 percent of full-time first-year students at community colleges came from families with earnings below $20,000 as compared to 14 percent entering baccalaureate institutions (Carter, 1990). Community college students generally have lower socioeconomic backgrounds than those entering baccalaureate institutions (El-Khawas, Carter, and Ottinger, 1988). These students have the most to gain from a dominant collegiate function. Gains from the collegiate function would be important to middle-income students whose families have a history of college attendance; they are incredibly more valuable for poorer students new to the collegiate enterprise. To date, much of the community college rhetoric has extolled the virtues of providing educational gains for students, at least through the associate-degree level. A dominant collegiate function forces the community college to be more ambitious about its students.

The community college has thus far served both a horizontal and a vertical function. The horizontal function — reaching out and encompassing large numbers of individuals in a range of educational experiences — is a dominant theme in both the occupational and community service visions of the community college. The vertical function — reaching up and connecting to other institutional settings of likely importance to community college students — dominates the collegiate role. Educational attainment and personal mobility are tied to the ability to persist through various levels of higher education. Although it may be different one day, these gains are not realizable through the various horizontal functions.

There is a tension between the horizontal and vertical functions. The horizontal function tends to be identified with access and inclusion, while the vertical function is identified with selectivity and exclusion. Students do not proceed to senior institutions without judgments being made about their ability and potential; sorting takes place based on their prior performance. The tension is the result of confusing the conditions required for the horizontal function with those needed for the vertical function when they are not the same. The horizontal function may or may not require college-level skills of students, but college-level skills are essential for the vertical function; they are critical to achieving the baccalaureate degree. The horizontal function may or may not require the establishment of educational goals toward which students persist over time; this is essential to the vertical function. The horizontal function may or may not require knowledgeable use of various bureaucratic structures; the vertical function requires this information. Students cannot be assured that behaviors that produce success in the horizontal function will produce success in the vertical function. Because the horizontal function is the primary participation arena of the community college, the vertical function, which requires alternative behaviors that might discourage participation, is sometimes suspect.

Gain Two: Serving Society
Through Serving Nontraditional Students

The most important — and perhaps least addressed — challenge to the educational community in the last twenty years is the changing attendance patterns of students coupled with their changing demographics. These students are called nontraditional;

they are considered nontraditional by virtue of their attendance patterns or personal characteristics: they are part-time, non-degree, older, female, minority, poorer, or working. Ross and Hampton point out that of all the descriptors, attendance patterns, especially part-time attendance, affect students and institutions the most (Eaton, 1992b). Nondegree status is significant as well. Part-time attendance that does not culminate in a degree removes students from many of the academic requirements of the college and university. Unless other strategies have been used to organize students' educational investment, nondegree status enables them to opt out of sequential learning experiences.

Nontraditional students are in the majority. According to data from the 1987 National Study of Postsecondary Aided Students (NPSAS), nontraditional students, identified by the attendance patterns and personal descriptors above, made up almost 12 million of the 17 million college and university attendees in 1987, or more than 70 percent. In community colleges, they comprised 6.2 million of the 7.5 million credit enrollees, or more than 80 percent.

Part-time students are a particularly large group within the nontraditional student population. Ross and Hampton's analysis of the NPSAS data indicates that 66.2 percent of students in public colleges, 77 percent in two-year schools, and 51 percent in four-year schools are part-time students (Eaton, 1992b). The NPSAS data include enrollments throughout the academic year. Alternative data that include only fall enrollments report part-time students to be 43.3 percent of all enrollments. In the community college, they make up the majority of enrollments, or 64.2 percent; in four-year institutions, they make up 30.8 percent of enrollments (National Center for Education Statistics, 1991). The percentage of nontraditional students who are nondegree is not clear from either data set.

Given the enormous presence of nontraditional students in the community college, one of the greatest contributions the community college can make to society is to realize its potential as the country's most important site of nontraditional education. Nontraditional students—especially part-time and nondegree students—who are likely to attend community colleges are often seeking a traditional collegiate education. With more and more of these students in higher education, a collegiate community college offering quality college-level studies that are structured to meet nontraditional needs can provide valuable educational leadership for the country. Models showing an effective marriage between collegiate programs and the needs of part-time and other nontraditional students are badly needed—and the community college is the richest site for their development. The educational niche that the community college can occupy in the future is as a site where nontraditional students can pursue a collegiate experience offered in a nontraditional mode.

A dominant collegiate function focused on nontraditional students will ensure that its structured, sequential, college-level liberal arts and career education programs will also include structures for part-time students and nondegree students. It will strengthen the relationship between faculty and nontraditional students and provide administrative leadership to establish curricular structures and encourage this faculty role. The community college, for all its rhetoric about the nontraditional student, still, for the most part, develops curricula as if they will be used by full-time, degree-seeking students and provides support services based on the same assumption. A dominant collegiate function that adequately attends to nontraditional students cannot be fashioned on the pattern of the traditional full-time, degree-seeking student. It needs to be developed according to the actual attendance and educational goal patterns of the students—or else student behavior must be changed.

Curricular Structure for Nontraditional Students. Building a dominant collegiate function that is nontraditional requires an approach to curricular structure that focuses on the part-time attendance patterns of the students. The traditional collegiate structure includes associate-degree programs that are completed in two to four years. Students are assumed to attend full-time and without either work or family responsibilities that might interfere with their studies. Ross and Hampton's analysis shows that only 23 percent of the students in public community colleges can accurately be described in this manner (Eaton, 1992b).

When students attend part-time, their educational experience usually involves unstructured enrollment in courses, which is an unsatisfactory form of curricular organization.

Four developments in the curricular structure are needed to accommodate these students: (1) multiyear curricular paths that lead to a degree, (2) curricular structures for studies that do not culminate in a degree but do involve some other sort of recognition such as a certificate, (3) curricular structures for transfer that are built across institutions, and (4) curricular structures that accommodate simultaneous pursuit of education and work. In the first instance, shifting to multiyear curricular paths acknowledges that the two-year time sequence for degree programs is no longer especially helpful. The degree programs that are used should be offered in varying time intervals from three to ten years. These longer time intervals provide structure for part-time students and can be undertaken without affecting their family and work responsibilities.

For example, a student enrolling in a career program in social service would develop, with faculty and counselors, a five-year plan to pursue either a specific number of sequential courses in the program area or an associate degree in applied science. This plan would call for the student to complete certain courses during each semester and would even allow for skipping a semester if necessary. The student would still be able to work, either full- or part-time. Partway through the plan, the student could structure a second phase of education for transfer and eventual receipt of the baccalaureate degree. This second phase would also accommodate work and other responsibilities. A similar educational plan could be developed in liberal arts with the option of the associate of arts degree. These long-term education plans are, in fact, being followed by many students. What is needed is for the institutions that they are attending to take additional responsibility for structuring and guiding the educational plan.

Part-time attendance for students who have educational goals other than a degree requires action based on the same principles used for structuring long-term educational plans ending in degrees. First, the unstructured enrollment in courses characteristic of so many community college students needs to be organized in a sequenced structure. Enrollment in courses must move from an ad hoc activity to an organized educational experience with a goal. The cluster approach taken by some community colleges and the credit-bearing interdisciplinary units that have been developed at others are examples of these goal-oriented, sequenced learning experiences. Second, the sequences or structures should be developed with part-time students in mind. It is self-defeating for an institution to replace expectations of full-time enrollment in degree programs with expectations of full-time enrollment in a sequence of offerings that fall short of a degree.

Curricular structures that allow transfer and accommodate work schedules involve similar organizational considerations. The structures must go beyond institutional boundaries, from two-year to four-year institutions or from the two-year institution to the workplace, and curricular paths must be developed that take into account changes in the location of educational offerings, shifting the perception that the educational experience is confined to the community college. This may extend the transfer function beyond the linear path from the two-year to the four-year school to establish simultaneous enrollment and early recognition of the baccalaureate as an educational goal. In the case of education and work, educational experiences and work expectations should be developed in tandem. Instead of education and work being seen as conflicting with each other, they may be perceived as mutually reinforcing. A cross-institutional approach to setting educational goals can help deal with Adelman's concern (1992) that successful "occasional" use of the community college by students precludes its effectiveness as a collegiate institution. A more structured occasional use and firm educational goals should bode well for the collegiate function.

Relationships Between Faculty and Nontraditional Students. Beyond the curriculum, building a dominant collegiate function for nontraditional students depends heavily on the faculty. Faculty interest in students as demonstrated by time spent in and out of classes, faculty attitudes that value collegiate education and support the baccalaureate degree, and faculty commitment to college-level performance standards all can help the nontraditional student to successfully pursue traditional academic education.

The part-time attendance patterns of nontraditional students gives classroom faculty the greatest opportunity for contact with these individuals. Part-time attendance, especially when it is coupled with the community college's tendency to allow students to choose their courses and failures to enforce prerequisites, contributes to the likelihood that community college students will spend little time with counselors or other student support personnel. Teaching faculty can make use of this powerful opportunity to help students focus on longer-range educational goals that go beyond the community college. They can play an important role as mentors and models for students, helping them to develop programs of study that fit their nontraditional circumstances.

Additionally, integrating counseling and advising services with classroom instruction and flexibly assigning faculty and counselors to teaching, advising, and counseling roles are essential to creating a dominant collegiate function that is effective for these students. This can culminate in the development of models to help nontraditional and especially part-time students by augmenting more traditional counseling and advising services that are isolated from the classroom experience. Faculty can agree to advising part-time students on an individual or group basis. Faculty and counselors can agree to dismantle an arbitrary division of labor in which faculty are confined to teaching and counselors are confined to advice and assistance. Counselors can be an ongoing part of the classroom experience.

A programmatic structure can also be useful in building faculty support for part-time students. If students enroll in a cluster of courses or a limited number of credits that constitute a structured, sequential learning experience with which faculty are identified, a community of teaching and learning is formed in which the students can feel at home. Students may feel more comfortable about turning to faculty for assistance, and faculty are more likely to come to know students on an individual basis. Again, counselors can be part of the teaching-learning community.

As with any significant change in a community college, administrative support and financing is essential. Administrative leadership is especially critical. This can be achieved by encouraging the development of models of relationships between faculty and part-time students in which administrators can become better informed about the needs of part-time and other nontraditional students. A dominant collegiate function for nontraditional students also requires administrative awareness that the majority of students are using the community college in ways that are significantly different than they were at the time when many faculty job descriptions were developed. As with the curricular structure, faculty responsibilities should reflect an obligation to nontraditional students, and the administration should take a fresh look at the relationship between students' needs and the shape and substance of the faculty's work.

Gain Three: Enrichment and Intellectual Legitimacy for the Institution

A dominant collegiate function enriches the two-year college, making it intellectually stronger and more viable. This can occur in at least two ways. First, making the collegiate function dominant will both reinforce the importance of collegiate faculty to the institution and enlarge their role. Second, it can bring community colleges into national conversations about important intellectual issues in higher education, such as the value of general education and the effects of multiculturalism. In the 1980s in particular, community colleges were virtually absent from many important academic conversations including discussion of academic reform and assessment in higher education. Although there was some community college representation in the groups that produced, for example *Involvement in Learning* (Study Group on the Condition of Excellence in American Higher Education, 1984), *To Reclaim a Legacy* (Bennett, 1984), and *Integrity in the College Curriculum* (Association of American Colleges, 1985), the community college had a minimal presence in the important discussions these works engendered. This was a loss to the community college's professional staff and the students they served as well as to the higher education community, which did not have the advantage of community college perspectives on key issues. Participation in national dialogues enriches faculty and administrators and, ultimately, the students they assist.

The State of the Faculty. As of 1987, community colleges employed 256,236 faculty. Of these, 107,608 were full-time (Cohen and Brawer, 1989). Full-time faculty have primary responsibility for teaching in degree-credit programs. Liberal arts faculty make up more than half of the full-time community college classroom personnel. Faculty have a strong interest in college-level learning, pursue various forms of scholarship, and have some connection with their disciplines. They are, in many ways, the guardians of the intellectual worth of the community college.

Community college faculty, however, are a somewhat disaffected and discouraged group of professionals (Cohen and Brawer, 1987; McGrath and Spear, 1991; Palmer and Vaughan, 1992; Richardson, Fisk, and Okun, 1983; Seidman, 1985). Over the years, they have found themselves shunted aside because of administrative interest in community services or vocational training programs. They have been pressured to relax collegiate standards to accommodate underprepared students and have had the most difficult teaching assignments in higher education: teaching classes of students who vary greatly in levels of academic preparedness and interest. These faculty do not have the benefit of the screening or selective admission of students that results in more homogenous classrooms with better-prepared students. Collegiate faculty, through their senates and unions, may be politically powerful within their institutions, but their academic authority has been diminished in the face of the compelling influence of vocational training programs and noncredit courses. Making the collegiate function central would have the effect of reinvigorating the faculty and their academic authority. This would have the effect of greatly enhancing the academic life of the community college.

Seidman (1985), in one of the first studies of the community college faculty since Cohen and Brawer's 1977 study, talks about a faculty loss of control and ties it to several factors, including the diminishing of the collegiate function over time. The replacement of traditional liberal arts courses with "noncollegiate" efforts such as remedial, occupational, and outreach (noncredit) offerings caused uneasiness among faculty. He also identifies the leveling-off of enrollments in the 1970s and 1980s as a factor. Growth in enrollments, he argues, brought a sense of unlimited horizons to faculty efforts. Without this expansion in the student population, faculty were constrained by the bureaucracy and centralization of increased administrative control. Seidman further maintains that community college faculty sustain a nagging sense of inferiority caused by the perception that they are at the bottom of a higher education hierarchy. They carry out their work in an environment of fragmented curricula, inequitable collegial relations, and the belief that they have a low educational status.

Many of Seidman's suggestions for lessening faculty discouragement involve the collegiate function. He calls for further integration of the occupational and liberal arts, an increased emphasis on writing, a smaller commitment to objective testing, encouragement for students to take more responsibility for their own learning, support for faculty pursuing the doctorate, and strengthened support and commitment to faculty scholarship. He makes a strong case for enhancing the intellectual life of the community college:

> What became more and more clear in the interviews was that for faculty . . . learning was a source of power and opportunity. It was clear from the interviews that if the intellectual center of teachers' work were to be recognized, priorities in the community college as a whole would be restructured and faculty and students alike would be empowered as a result. Intellectual work cuts across rank, curricula, gender, race, social class, and place on the community college totem pole. Intellectual work was seen by faculty as the source of renewal and continued energy for doing their work. If the com-

munity college can become a place in which societal ambivalence toward intellectual work is left at
the front door, then both students and faculty will
experience a sense of opportunity that can give new
meaning to community college education and to the
work of community college faculty [p. 276].

The current interest in scholarship in the community college (Palmer, 1994; Palmer and Vaughan, 1992; Vaughan,
1988; Vaughan and Palmer, 1991) can be a powerful base of
support for a dominant collegiate function as a means to intellectual enrichment. Palmer talks about the "unfinished nature of
the community college teacher's professional identity" in relation to both teaching and disciplinary scholarship (Palmer, 1994,
p. 424). His review of the literature on faculty confirms that
classroom teaching dominates professional life although, all too
frequently, it is not "purposeful teaching toward defined ends
and at collegiate levels" (p. 428). This is compounded by what
faculty perceive to be antagonism by institutional culture toward
scholarly endeavors outside the classroom. Scholarly efforts are
seen as diminishing the commitment to teaching.
        Palmer points out that scholarly demands on faculty may
grow, perhaps as a result of an emphasis on curricular reform or
the assessment movement. Further, efforts to redefine scholarship (Boyer, 1990; Vaughan, 1988) may have an impact on the
community college. These scholarly demands may be discipline-
based, thus contributing to a growth of interest in the liberal
arts in the community college as well as to interest in its connection with four-year institutions. He urges further examination of the community college environment in relation to scholarship and to faculty self-perceptions of their obligations and
asks whether adequate emphasis is being placed on documented
student learning as distinct from "student-centeredness"—a concern raised by Seidman (1985) and Richardson, Fisk, and Okun
(1983) as well. Student-centeredness has to do with the personal
relationships faculty develop with students. But as important
as this is, it cannot replace a strong commitment to documented
student learning.

Vaughan (1988) explicitly links scholarship in the community college to participation in the larger higher education community. He defines scholarship for the community college as systematic pursuit of a topic, or objective, rational inquiry. For Vaughan, research is only one form of scholarship. In a manner similar to Boyer's (Boyer, 1990), Vaughan calls for various forms of scholarship that can result in a variety of products, such as book reviews, annotated bibliographies, lectures, or syntheses of existing research. He calls scholarship the avenue through which we stay in touch with the academic enterprise. Community colleges need scholarship for legitimacy in higher education. According to Vaughan, "Scholarship in academia is truly the coin of the realm for without it, we might as well be working with the local bank or department store" (p. 29f).

Vaughan's definition of scholarship became the foundation for a national survey by the Center for Community College Education at George Mason University in 1991 (Palmer and Vaughan, 1992). Using Vaughan's definition, Palmer found that 86 percent of full-time faculty and 75 percent of part-time faculty had engaged in scholarly activity during the previous two years. Full- and part-time faculty received some encouragement for their efforts (37 percent of full-time and 26 percent of part-time faculty). Fewer enjoyed financial support (15 percent of full-time and 6 percent of part-time faculty). A number received no help at all (27 percent of full-time and 50 percent of part-time faculty). Although faculty in the survey indicated that scholarly work would enhance their teaching effectiveness, they cited limited time, limited financial resources, and limited support as significant barriers to this activity. They also saw this work as optional and personal rather than as an institutionalized professional obligation.

For the future, Palmer calls for a refinement of Boyer and Vaughan's expanded definition of scholarship, urging that these activities are *potentially* scholarly. He also points out that an expanded definition of scholarship such as Vaughan's will require time to become accepted. Many faculty in the survey still view research and publication as the primary forms of scholarly effort.

Palmer urges further encouragement and support of faculty efforts through an institutional culture that values their work. This can have the effect of making scholarship institutionally important and removing it from the realm of the personal and optional.

Intellectual Enrichment: Participating in the Higher Education Community. Although higher education is highly complex and decentralized, it does form a loosely connected intellectual community, in which issues of importance to educators are discussed and debated. In the 1980s, for example, these issues included academic reform and assessment. Issues such as general education and the quality of teaching have a long history of debate and discussion. Periodically, higher education becomes concerned with managerial effectiveness. Since the 1960s, educators have been especially concerned with diversity, particularly diversity of race and gender. As viewed in various influential publications, national and regional meetings, and the higher education literature, the community college has not been an active participant in this national intellectual community and its conversations.

Higher education, in the early 1990s, has continued its national conversations through a series of debates about the content of education, the norms of scholarship, and the authority of the college and university in regulating campus life. These debates are important because they go to the heart of the academic enterprise: the nature and structure of the curricula that students will study, the values to which they will be exposed on campus, and the attitudes that will be demonstrated toward fundamental beliefs in the society such as freedom of expression and social justice. Although these issues are of prime importance to the community college as well as to four-year institutions, the community college, once again, has not been an ongoing participant in the debates.

The first of these recent debates, about what is sometimes called political correctness, is a confusing quarrel about the way diversity is valued on college campuses — what the official campus culture signals students to believe about, for example, racial minorities, women, individuals with disabilities, and homosexuals. The issues at stake include campus practices such as affirmative action in admission, preferential hiring of faculty and administration, and special protection for minorities and others once they are on campus. The argument is that those who speak for the rights of minorities, women, and others and against what they perceive as white, male norms of behavior have forced their views on the campus as a whole. Second, it is alleged that these spokespersons have tyrannized students into sharing their beliefs or at least have been so intimidating that students are hesitant to challenge the beliefs taught in the classroom and on the campus. This quarrel is about both the beliefs that are held and the extent to which some people attempt to impose those beliefs on students and campuses.

The second debate, about free speech, focuses on the regulatory dimension of dealing with diversity. It is a difference of opinion about how to prevent, for example, racist, sexist, and homophobic behavior on campus, particularly in speech. The quarrel emerged when changes in the student population to include more minorities produced conflict on campus, an inhospitable climate for minorities, and overtly racist and sexist acts. On one side are those who recommend regulating speech through the establishment of codes, on the theory that regulation of expression will produce decency of thought. On the other side are those who feel that regulation violates constitutional rights to free speech. At its zenith, the quarrel embraced the notion that the traditional interpretation of the Bill of Rights of the Constitution as intended to protect individuals should be reinterpreted to protect groups.

The third and most important debate, multiculturalism, is ostensibly about curricular content. At its core, however, it involves a dispute about whether or not the primary purpose of the curriculum is academic or political. This is a difference of opinion between those scholars who see the curriculum as conveying values and judgments about social conditions and those who see it as an arena of intellectual inquiry first and a vehicle for social commentary second. The first group contends that the curriculum is a vehicle for creating the society they deem desirable. The second group operates on the notion that the curriculum functions as a source of inquiry and discussion; although values and judgments are conveyed by the curriculum, they can be identified without being used to influence the social views of students. This group emphasizes the academic purpose of the curriculum, while the first group emphasizes the political purpose of the curriculum; they view the context in which intellectual inquiry takes place as dispositive about what the curriculum teaches, rather than subscribing to the notion that independent rational inquiry by the student will enable him or her to make judgments about the nature of the curriculum.

Multiculturalism refers, simultaneously and confusingly, to (1) unintegrated additions to the curriculum that are not focused on the United States or Europe, (2) a special emphasis on African studies, and (3) efforts to forge a new curriculum that synthesizes Western and other traditions in a manner that reflects the needs of the heterogeneous society in which we live along with a willingness to be constructively critical of Western institutions.

Ravitch (1990) describes the debate as a conflict between two approaches: pluralistic and particularistic multiculturalism. Pluralists seek a common culture, while particularists believe that a common culture is not possible. The particularists are especially focused on an ethnocentric curriculum, believing it to be desirable for racial minorities. The pluralists believe that a common culture can exist that is informed by ethnic differences. Ravitch talks about education in this country as "Americentric" (p. 348), or centered on itself. Schlesinger (1992), commenting on the debate, characterizes the multicultural struggle as a difference of opinion between those who see the future of society as an essentially balkanized federation of cultures and those who see it as requiring some cohesion of values, beliefs, and perceptions. He says, "'Multiculturalism' arises as a reaction against Anglo- or Eurocentrism; but at what point does it pass over into an ethnocentrism of its own?" (p. 74). He believes that it is one result of racial and ethnic pressures on the schools. To the extent that it fosters ethnic exclusivity, Schlesinger is troubled: "Instead of a transformative nation with an identity all its own, America in this new light is seen as preservative of diverse alien identities" (p. 16).

Cohen, one of the few community college educators commenting on this issue, sees multiculturalism as an attack on "reading as a dominant form of apprehending information and ideas" (Cohen, personal communication, April 1992). It is an assault on print, on the repository of accumulated knowledge as our society has created it, contrasted with the immediacy of the visual. Recall the Vietnam War and the impact of television. This is instant apprehension, but it does not contribute to linear discourse and rationality. Cohen comments:

> In academe we try to build curriculum that recognizes the contributions, values, and uniqueness of each ethnic group and we effect affirmative action policies to ensure that each group is represented proportionately in the faculty and the student body. But the closer we get to equality of condition, the more difficult it becomes to explain unequal outcomes. If we are truly just, why do all groups not participate and achieve at the same rate? Obviously we are either unjust or all groups are not equal. Since we cannot consider the latter in open forum, we continually seek evidence of the former, whether overt, covert, mystical, or psychological.

Virtually none of the major general works written about political correctness, free speech, and multiculturalism were authored by community college educators. The major general publications of higher education such as *Educational Record* and *Change* do not include the reflections of community college educators on these topics, and scholarly journals also reflect their absence. The major community college publications such as the *Community, Technical, and Junior College Journal* and the *Community College Review* fail to address these issues.

Of the debates discussed above, the multicultural discussion is likely to have the most lasting significance. At the campus level, the research to date shows that community colleges are much less engaged in multicultural issues than four-year institutions (El-Khawas, 1992; Levine and Cureton, 1992). Levine and Cureton undertook a random survey of 270 institutions through a questionnaire sent to chief academic officers or deans of faculty. While questions can be raised about the methodology of the survey, it is, to date, the only available indication of activity in two- and four-year institution's in relation to these issues. The survey, which received responses from 196 institutions, or 72.6 percent, focuses on the involvement of the institutions in multicultural activities, including general education, support services, curricular development, and recruitment and retention. Levine and Cureton stipulate: "The inescapable conclusion is that multiculturalism is widespread in higher education today. . . . a quiet revolution of sorts. . . . activity has not been systematic or well-defined" (p. 29).

With regard to community colleges, Levine and Cureton found that for all the dimensions of multiculturalism addressed in the survey, community colleges were simply less engaged in the range of activities for which the researchers sought responses. A smaller percentage of community colleges had multicultural general education requirements, courses in ethnic and gender studies, changes in the disciplines, faculty programs, advising, or centers and institutes, despite housing a more diverse student population.

El-Khawas (1992), in her annual survey of campus administrators to determine campus trends, confirms Levine and Cureton's findings. When they were asked whether or not multicultural perspectives are reflected in the general education curriculum, only 63 percent of community colleges answered affirmatively, compared to 76 percent of all institutions and 85 percent of doctoral granting institutions. Only 15 percent of community colleges indicated that they require specific courses that focus on multicultural issues, compared to 31 percent of all institutions and 51 percent of baccalaureate institutions. Fifty-six percent of community colleges said that these courses are offered, although they may not be required; this compares to 69 percent of all institutions and 84 percent of doctoral institutions. Only when they were asked whether multicultural material is included as a part of general courses did community colleges show greater involvement. Eighty-two percent answered affirmatively, compared to 84 percent of all institutions and 89 percent of baccalaureate institutions. Fewer doctoral institutions —

71 percent—said yes. This trend held for racial and ethnic studies, non-western studies, and women's studies. It also held when institutions were asked about course revisions that would include a multicultural perspective in humanities, the social sciences, and the natural sciences. On the positive side, some courses are being revised and multicultural changes are being discussed at a number of institutions.

Summary

This chapter has explored the case for a collegiate community college. It described a dominant collegiate function in some detail, acknowledging that the core concept of college-level study can, at best, be described with limited precision. It then explored the impact of a dominant collegiate role on the long-standing commitment of the community college to comprehensiveness and showed why advocating a dominant collegiate role is controversial. A dominant collegiate function will change the community college's commitment to comprehensiveness by forcing the collegiate purpose to be valued over the other three purposes that are generally associated with comprehensiveness: occupational education, developmental and remedial education, and community service. Advocating a dominant collegiate function is likely to be controversial because of its impact on comprehensiveness, its insistence on unambiguously identifying the community college with higher education, and its diminished commitment to precollege work.

As justification for challenging comprehensiveness and perhaps encouraging controversy, the chapter identified three major gains that result from making the collegiate function dominant: gains to the student, the society, and the institution itself. Students are virtually assured of greater educational attainment, increased earnings, and greater occupational status if they proceed beyond the associate degree to the baccalaureate or a more demanding career. Society gains from having a successful educational site of collegiate education for nontraditional students. The community colleges themselves gain through enrichment of their intellectual life and especially through revitalization of the community college faculty in both their teaching and their scholarship.

Chapter Seven

Reinforcing and Enhancing
the Collegiate Function

This chapter considers how the institutional agenda of the community college should be shaped and how institutional priorities should be ordered in order to sustain a dominant collegiate function. It also explores the desirability of repositioning the community college within the higher education enterprise as a way to build collegiate commitment. Making the collegiate role dominant requires changes in practice and policy and perhaps even in the fundamental structure of the community college as an autonomous, two-year institution.

Specifically, the chapter examines three areas of community college practice and policy that would have to be modified in order to make the collegiate function dominant. First, the associate degree must be strengthened or abandoned: it does not serve its primary function of structuring educational experiences for students. If strengthened, it will provide a framework for delivery of transferable liberal arts and career education offerings, two of the conditions essential to the collegiate community college. Second, general education must serve the collegiate function to a greater extent than it does now: it is an outstanding vehicle for creating the needed institutional culture—another of the conditions for a collegiate community college. It can help to address the difficult issue of defining college-level study as well. Third, the commitment to institutional access must be modified: it needs to be limited by restricting the scope of developmental and remedial studies on campus and requiring minimum competence for entry to college-level courses and programs. This is essential in order for the four conditions of the collegiate community college to prevail. These three areas of community college operation are addressed because they are central to any institution that seeks to create a dominant collegiate function.

While this chapter discusses the place of the community college within the higher education enterprise, it does not offer any conclusions about structural change for the community college. It does stress the importance of revisiting this discussion in the event that efforts to make the collegiate function dominant through operational changes are not successful.

This discussion of ways to shape the institutional agenda does not include specific examples of institutional practices for creating a dominant collegiate function. Instead, it relies on providing generic descriptions of actions that faculty and administrators might take. While there are many practices in the literature that are of value to a dominant collegiate function, their effectiveness has not been independently confirmed and it would be misleading to present them here.

Strengthening the Collegiate Function and the Community College as "Other Than"

Many of the suggestions offered here to make the collegiate function dominant are familiar; a number of them are controversial in that they call for a significant departure from the prevailing attitudes and beliefs that have guided decades of community college work and commitment. In general, these suggestions challenge the long-standing theme among community college educators that there is value in being different from traditional higher education, in being "other than," that has played through the history of both the junior college and community college.

Being "other than" means that the two-year institution invests heavily in programs and services that are different from those of four-year colleges and universities. The community college, the argument goes, is at its best when it is doing what traditional higher education does not do. Gleazer's community-based vision is an example of being "other than," as is Parnell's vocationalism and rejection of the baccalaureate goal. The commu- nity college's commendable commitment to instructional inno- vation, emphasis on nonpunitive grading, and formative ap- proach to evaluation — its student-centeredness — are examples of being "other than."

Making the collegiate role dominant will challenge the importance of being "other than." To be successful in asserting the collegiate role, community colleges will have to place addi- tional emphasis on their *similarity* to other higher education in- stitutions. In areas of curriculum, teaching, and learning, they will need to strengthen their relationships with other institutions, especially four-year receiving institutions. This should be done with the intention of establishing a sense of shared responsibil- ity for curricular content and standards in order to encourage similarities in other areas; it will replace the existing tendency toward superordinate-subordinate relationships in which the community college is dominated by the four-year school. To deal with public perception and financing, community colleges will need to establish academic legitimacy or affirm the worth of enrolling in the community college for collegiate purposes and of investing in the community college as a public good. Es- pecially in the 1970s and 1980s, community colleges tended to be valued for their commitment to access and occupational edu- cation rather than for their collegiate role. Well-meaning citizens talked about community college students moving on to "real" college or "regular" college after the community college. This sense that the community college is not firmly part of higher education needs to change in order to establish a central colle- giate function.

Moving away from investment in "other than" does not require community colleges to completely reject the qualities that set them apart from the rest of higher education. It does require them to make a significant additional investment in the areas in which they are similar to the four-year and university world. Community college presidents and the national leader- ship need to value similarity, invest importance in the collegiate function, and strengthen relationships with the other higher edu- cation institutions with which they work.

Institutional Investment in the Collegiate Role

The collegiate role has been around for so long that it is treated like a live-in relative the family has stopped noticing. It was the "given" handed to junior colleges and did not have to be developed or justified in the same way as other junior and community college functions. When community college presidents are asked whether they support the collegiate function, they insist that they do and point to it as part of the comprehensive mission of their institutions. Frequently, however, they have not looked at the collegiate function in a long time. Because of its longevity, they assume that it is doing just fine. Acknowledging the collegiate function but not paying special attention to it has had a negative effect; it has resulted in the collegiate function becoming less important than other functions. The institution is not creatively managing the collegiate function and its value is not conveyed adequately to students. When community college presidents, faculty, and boards of trustees pay no attention to the collegiate function, they allow it to wither away.

The Role of the President, the Faculty, and the Board

Presidents, along with faculty and boards of trustees, carry the primary responsibility for successful institutional investment in the collegiate role. The president sets a collegiate agenda, the board develops policies that provide a framework for it, and the faculty offer intellectual leadership in curricular development, pedagogy, and academic standards. Board policies, strategic plans, statements of mission, and budgets that consistently support the collegiate function all provide the foundation for this institutional investment.

When a president sets an agenda that makes the collegiate function dominant, he or she provides direction, encourages the values needed to invest in the collegiate function, and acts as the primary advocate for collegiate work. It is the president's particular responsibility to make the collegiate function more important to the institution, to manage it creatively, and to ensure that its values are conveyed to students. This can be done through strategic plans that affirm the collegiate function as the primary institutional responsibility. As discussed in Chapter Four, academic policy deliberations with faculty and academic administrators can confirm the importance of a strong collegiate function. Institutional self-scrutiny can ensure that all enabling documents that speak to the institution's vision, aims, purposes, and mission are dedicated to the collegiate function. The president's efforts, if successful, provide the essential foundation for focusing institutional energy on the collegiate role.

The faculty make the collegiate function dominant through leadership in developing college-level course content and academic standards and through their encouragement to students to set long-range educational goals. Activities such as developing curricula, pursuing scholarly applied research, building relationships with other higher education institutions, and developing support services that are specifically focused on college-level studies are major elements of a strong faculty role in building the collegiate function. New curricular initiatives should be college-level, faculty development programs should address collegiate studies, and applied research should focus on college-level work and institutional assessment. The faculty need support when they work with other institutions of higher education to strengthen the transfer function and when they engage in scholarly activity that meaningfully involves them in the larger higher education world. Similarly, academic administrators need to be supported and encouraged to engage in some of these activities.

The community college's governing board should provide a policy framework for the president and faculty. It is the president's responsibility to persuade the board of trustees that this is essential. The board, in turn, provides leadership for a dominant collegiate function by approving budgets and endorsing strategic plans that incorporate this priority. Boards can and should reject planning and budgeting that do not include a primary collegiate function. They can develop incentive programs for faculty and academic administrators that strengthen the collegiate function and can expand their presence at the local, state, and national levels by demonstrating their advocacy for a dominant collegiate function among other trustees at two- and four-year institutions. Boards can undertake development activities that build their leadership skills for the collegiate function.

Structured, Sequential Education and the Associate Degree

The associate degree can play a major role in making the collegiate function dominant in the community college. At present, the associate degree is not a major factor in community college education and it is badly in need of attention, not only in relation to a dominant collegiate function but also as part of a general assessment of its use and purpose within the community college. The associate degree is the primary means of guiding students into sequential, structured learning. If it is not effective at this task, another method is needed to achieve an organized educational experience. Structuring of educational experiences is critical to the success of liberal arts and career education offerings and their transferability—two key concerns of a collegiate community college. If the degree is available but not used, it should not be continued. Under these circumstances, the presence of the degree functions as an excuse to avoid addressing the need for structuring the student experience.

The degree dates back to 1873. With the University of Chicago's decision in 1900 to award the associate degree in arts, literature, and science, it became a standard feature of junior college development (Lombardi, 1980). Originally created as an appropriate marker of junior college completion, the associate degree became, within the community college, the organizing principle for programs and curricula. Lombardi notes that the associate degree has been widely accepted by community colleges since 1945, citing the number of degrees awarded annually and the extent to which various occupational areas and discipline-based studies have used it to seek recognition. The degree's position as an organizing principle was undermined by the student choice movement of the 1960s, when student judgment about degree requirements became as important as institutional judgment. Degrees such as the associate of general studies could be earned, not through structured programs, but by undertaking any of a number of different courses selected by students.

Efforts to reestablish the importance of the associate degree — at least for occupational programs — were undertaken by Dale Parnell and the AACC in the mid 1980s. In 1984, the AACC adopted an "Associate Degree Preferred" policy statement that called for increased use of the degree for occupational programs (Parnell, 1985a). Although the policy statement reaffirmed the associate degree as "central to the mission of two-year colleges," the campaign has not been accompanied by increases in associate-degree acquisition. To the contrary, since 1984, the number of degrees has declined: the American Association of Community and Junior Colleges (1991) reports that 452,416 associate degrees were awarded in 1984; by 1990, this had diminished to 444,953. They do not provide data on occupational associate degrees, although this degree was the primary focus of the campaign.

The bigger picture is not encouraging, either. Although associate-degree acquisition increased from 360,171 degrees in 1975 to 444,953 in 1990 (American Association of Community and Junior Colleges, 1991), it did not significantly increase as a percentage of enrollments. In 1975, 4,069,279 students enrolled in public and private community colleges and approximately 8 percent received degrees; an estimated 5,851,953 students enrolled in 1990 and approximately 9 percent received degrees. The number of associate degrees increased by 20 percent while enrollments increased by almost 40 percent. The percentage of students who receive associate degrees is inflated because the statistics include associate degrees earned at four-year institutions and at two-year schools that are not accredited community colleges. These schools are estimated to account for at least 50,000 degrees per year (Cohen, 1985–1986).

The associate degree does not appear to be a degree of choice for students in liberal arts curricula. Although the data are extremely limited, students who use liberal arts programs to transfer do not rely heavily on the associate degree. Major efforts undertaken in the last decade to strengthen the transfer function place little emphasis on acquisition of the associate degree. In California, for example, the associate degree is not even a requirement for admission to either California State

University or the University of California. The most extensive longitudinal study to date of community college students, the National Longitudinal Study of the High School Class of 1972, indicates that the associate degree is a weak force, earned by only 20 percent of 1972 graduates who attended a community college between 1972 and 1984 (Adelman, 1992).

An important recent effort to assess the impact of the associate degree at the state level was undertaken by James Palmer and Marilyn Pugh at George Mason University in Fairfax, Virginia (Palmer and Pugh, 1993), who tried to determine the role of the community college in attainment of the baccalaureate degree from Virginia's public universities. Analyzing the transcripts of baccalaureate-degree recipients during 1989–90, Palmer and Pugh describe the portion of the recipients who were transfer students and, among this group, the number of credits transfered from the community college, whether or not the transfer students earned the associate degree, and the programs to which they transferred. Palmer and Pugh could identify only 15 percent of the baccalaureate-degree recipients who transfered from a community college as also holding the associate degree. If this study were to be replicated in other states with similar findings, a case could be made that the associate degree is not a major factor in educational attainment. In addition to confirming that comparatively few students obtain the degree, evidence would show that it does not play a key role in sustaining the collegiate function.

For the future, community college educators need to explore whether or not it is beneficial for students to establish a strong relationship between the associate degree and the collegiate function. Does the associate degree matter? To answer this, community colleges need to do sufficient research to address three questions. First, does earning the associate degree confirm that students have realized the educational gains that might reasonably be associated with the completion of the second year of higher education? Second, does earning this degree produce economic and educational gains for occupational students that exceed the gains they would realize without the degree? Third, does earning this degree enhance the educational attainment of liberal arts and career education students who transfer compared to those who transfer without the degree?

Further, if the associate degree is found to be unimportant, community colleges need to find an alternative way to structure education and establish goals with students. Rejection of the associate degree should not be equivalent to rejection of sequential, structured learning experiences. Community colleges could develop a range of alternatives, including shorter-term educational experiences that culminate in some form of recognition and systems for officially structuring and sanctioning degree programs that greatly exceed two years to complete (see Chapter Six).

General Education

General education is a subject that has received comparatively little attention in the community college. An increase in its importance could enhance a dominant collegiate function. General education can be used as an important vehicle to help build a community college environment that values collegiate study, one of the four conditions for a collegiate community college, because attention to general education raises key questions about desired student competence as well as about the content and structure of the curriculum. A thorough conversation about general education encompasses significant questions concerning institutional intellectual values, the curriculum as a unifying experience, and academic standards.

General education was considered important to early junior college thinkers such as Lange (1918), Koos (1925), and Eells (1931a). The issues they addressed were different from contemporary concerns. Early junior college thinkers dealt primarily with terminal general education — what was needed for students who were pursuing neither occupational education nor specialized studies through transfer. Instead, their questions related to what today might be called civic education or education for citizens.

Community colleges have not continued the discussion of general education. Little of the contemporary conversations

in higher education about general education has caught the attention of community college educators. As described by the community college literature, general education, when it is addressed
at all, is part of a conversation about distribution requirements
or specially developed interdisciplinary or thematic coursework
related to degree attainment. Because of this, general education
requirements affect few community college students: the majority
have removed themselves from the influence of distribution requirements and take courses without receiving degrees. The few
interdisciplinary or thematic programs that have been developed
are positioned within degree programs for the minority of full-
time students and are not relevant to most students.

Johnson (1952, 1982) and Cohen and Brawer (1987, 1989)
have paid more attention to general education than other community college educators. Although Johnson's identification of
six approaches to general education (1952, 1982) is compelling
and challenging, his good thinking has not produced a large
number of general education programs in community colleges.
Cohen and Brawer (1987) provide an important service by defining general education specifically for the community college:
general education is made up of discipline-based courses designed to teach people to be enlightened citizens, the conversion of the liberal arts into something practical" (p. 11). They
see the liberal arts in the community college as "manifestations
of general education" (p. 171). Liberal arts courses are not "con-
templative" and "text-centered" as they might be in a four-year
environment, but their impact, too, has been limited.

At present, a few general education degree programs exist that are considered exciting models for the community college. These strategies are neither unusual nor challenging. Distribution requirements are the most important means of dealing
with general education (Cohen and Brawer, 1989). Interdisciplinary survey courses or integrated courses are widely offered,
especially in the humanities. Cross (1982) maintains that general
education has been part of the community college's mission but
that it has never been primary. Koltai (1982), focusing on the
transfer function, calls transfer-oriented general education a
"plight . . . that has reached disaster proportions." He argues

for a definition of general education that focuses on skills—the
"safety net of knowledge"—that students need to move to a four-
year institution. Students who transfer should have a general
education background that signals a certain level of competency.

The few current suggestions to strengthen general education in the community college reinforce the importance of
general education to a dominant collegiate function. Gaff, for
example, suggests that community colleges need to focus on quality, the liberal arts, and their collegiate role in the context of
an emphasis on general education. He maintains that community colleges must educate their respective markets to accept
more demanding requirements and the structured, coherent
educational experiences that make up a quality general education program (Raisman, 1993). Raisman (1993) urges the establishment of a solid general education information base as a
foundation for institutional decision making. Community colleges need to decide on the nature and extent of their commitment to general education, invest the necessary resources to build
a quality program, and educate the public about their offerings.

Changing Institutional Attitudes Toward Access

Those who view with alarm the development of a primary role
for the collegiate function are particularly worried that it will
result in limitations on access and that community colleges will
lose the special place they have created for themselves in American higher education as democracy's colleges. These alleged
negative effects deserve careful attention. A dominant collegiate
function will further restrict access, but this does not mean that
community colleges must cease to function as key access institutions in American higher education. As indicated in Chapter
Three, the community college has four kinds of access—academic, geographic, financial, and personal. The restrictions discussed here affect only academic access; the other forms of access
remain, thereby preserving the special place of the community
college.

In a dominant collegiate function, academic access should
be restricted in three ways. First, it should be restricted by ad-

ditional investment in the current community college practice of controlling enrollments. At present, some community college courses and programs are restricted to those students who demonstrate, at least at a minimum level, the needed competencies to undertake the work. A dominant collegiate function requires more of this access restriction.

No matter how open admission practices may be, the community college does sort and screen students. A collegiate community college will do this more extensively. Sorting and screening are the necessary means by which community colleges attempt, fairly and intelligently, to discriminate on the basis of demonstrated skill. These institutions need to ensure that testing, prerequisites, and other admissions screening procedures measure skills that are genuinely needed for college-level work. They also need to know that the procedures make a difference; they should ask: What would be the impact if the screening devices were not used? Would students admitted without these procedures do any worse than students who were screened? In addition, they need to make sure that these procedures are not contributing to unfair or illegal discrimination.

At the institutional level, most community colleges will admit all students for whom they have room; admission is the entry procedure certifying that a student may enroll in courses or programs under certain conditions. This institutional acceptance does not carry a guarantee of course or program acceptance. At the course level, a variety of devices are employed to limit access, including entrance tests to determine English and math skills that may affect whether or not a student may enter college-level coursework in certain areas. Psychology and sociology are available, for example, only to students who demonstrate college-level reading and writing skills.

At the program level, more elaborate screening devices are used. Especially in occupational areas, students frequently must meet certain cutoffs on standardized tests, have completed a range of college-level courses with a certain grade-point average, or have demonstrated proficiency through experiences such as creating portfolios or submitting writing samples. Many — if not all — of these limitations to access are sensible and defensible if students are to have some likelihood of success in their educational undertakings; however, they all constitute limitations. Ironically, occupational program areas have the most extensive constraints on access, although they are the most frequently cited as demonstrating the openness of the community college.

Even current developmental and remedial programs reflect limitations on access. Many community colleges have a floor for these programs, refusing to admit students whose level of remediation is below an institutionally established minimum. Some community colleges, for example, will not admit students who need remediation at an elementary school level of instruction. Diagnostic and other forms of testing are used to determine whether or not students can have access to developmental and remedial offerings.

The second way to restrict access is by further limiting developmental and remedial programs to only students with moderate remediation needs. *Moderate remediation needs* can be defined by individual institutions according to how much time they are willing to invest in preparing students for college-level work. It is reasonable, for example, to place a limit of two years or less on developmental work: if students who are not college-ready cannot acquire the skills needed for college-level work in this amount of time, they should not continue in the developmental coursework. Some effort will be needed to identify students' skill levels upon entry to developmental programs in order to ensure that they can achieve college-readiness within this time frame. More extensive remediation will need to be handled by other means such as the transition schools discussed later in this chapter.

The third way to restrict academic access is by making the development of college-level skills the specific focus of community college developmental efforts. This focus can connect developmental and remedial education to limited-access courses and programs by making preparation for college-level study the primary goal of developmental work. This is not, however, a substitute for adequate elementary and secondary education, and it will not resolve the problems of underprepared students who seek collegiate success. At most, it can modestly assist some students. The combination of limited access and college-focused developmental programs at the community college or four-year institutions has limited effectiveness for dealing with a large, seriously underprepared student population. These strategies must also be accompanied by a student tracking system that documents the educational attainment of individual students to ensure that the access-achievement connection is producing results.

Institutional attitudes toward access will change when the community college acknowledges, as has been argued here, that it is already a limited-access institution. At the course and program levels, this limited-access approach must be expanded to include more offerings. Admission to developmental and remedial courses must be confined to students with only moderate remediation needs. And the community college must use its developmental and remedial programs as the bridge between institutional access and program and course access, thus giving developmental work an exclusively college-level focus. This would be accompanied by a comprehensive program of student tracking to document educational attainment.

Connecting College-Level Studies with Other Programs

The above discussion of changing institutional attitudes toward access recommends acknowledging that the community college is a limited-access institution; establishing a consistent approach to access at the institutional, program, and course levels; and bringing a college-level focus to developmental programs. In addition to these important efforts, the community college can buttress its commitment both to the collegiate function and to access by ensuring that college-level studies are adequately connected to other college programs, whether they are developmental or vocational.

The collegiate function is sometimes portrayed as the community college's unfortunate and reluctant involvement with academic elitism. Successfully pursuing college-level work requires a minimum level of academic skill that not all students who attend community colleges may possess. Thus, a dominant collegiate function may be accompanied by two undesirable circumstances. It can result in exclusion of some students from programs that they might want to pursue, and it can produce a de facto tracking system, because those who cannot succeed at collegiate work are forced to pursue other programs if they wish to continue in the community college.

Through careful implementation of a strong collegiate function, the community college can reduce the likelihood that these undesirable circumstances will prevail. If the collegiate function is to take on a primary role in the community college, the institution should take steps to diminish the risk of elitism, avoid engaging in exclusionary practices, and discourage tracking that will harm students. Consistent curricular distribution requirements across all programs, integration of programs, and student assessment techniques that are appropriate for the diverse community college population are essential here. Many of the suggestions discussed below are already in practice in a number of community colleges. Expansion of these practices is essential to putting the collegiate function first—but in the right way.

Consistent curricular distribution requirements are the same for all degrees and certificates, whether students focus on the liberal arts, career education, the associate of arts area, or the associate of applied science area. A number of community colleges have different distribution requirements depending on the program in which a student is enrolled. Associate of arts degrees may have more demanding distribution requirements than associate of applied science degrees. This produces curricula with multiple standards that, in turn, yield a tracking system that can harm students by forcing some of them into coursework that demands too little. Intellectual opportunity is lost as a result of an erroneous belief that curricular choice conclusively describes student ability. A student in an occupational program should not be viewed as automatically unqualified to master college-level distribution requirements.

Liberal arts and career education distribution requirements are separately maintained in two ways. Course requirements may be diluted as in some cases where the liberal arts are watered down in the service of occupational programs, and substitutions in institutional distribution requirements may be allowed—for example, with Business English replacing first-year English or Biology for Nursing replacing first-year biology. Such decisions effectively bar students in these programs from successfully competing in a collegiate environment in the future. A college's distribution requirements should require collegiate work of *all* students obtaining an associate degree or participating in an associate-degree program. Collegiate coursework should be the intellectual foundation for all programs and degrees in the institution, with the exception of developmental and remedial work or special nondegree training efforts.

Program integration, or an emphasis on the interconnection among different levels of education, is also essential if emphasizing the collegiate function is done without tracking. In most institutions, the world of college-level liberal arts and career education is separate from the world of developmental and remedial work. The faculty are different, the funding is sometimes different, and the students are different. Developmental and remedial studies may not even be part of an academic division or department, but instead may be housed in the student services area.

Although much rhetoric is devoted to the movement of students from developmental and remedial programs to college-level work, comparatively few students really do this. The persistence and graduation rate for developmental students in community colleges is 24.0 percent. The rate for two-year technical colleges is higher, at 33.7 percent. *Persistence* is defined as still being enrolled after 3.5 years. This enrollment does not have to be in college-level courses (Boylan and Bonham, 1992); the practical effect of developmental and remedial programs on many students is to preclude their entry into the mainstream of community college work.

To change this situation, institutions can integrate developmental and remedial work with college-level work in two ways. First, students can enroll, where appropriate, in both levels of courses simultaneously. A student may need some developmental math, for example, but also be capable of college-level

English. If this is not feasible, a student's interest in moving into college-level work from developmental work can be ascertained early and ties with specific program areas or departments can be developed as preparation for future college-level enrollment. Developmental and remedial students can be helped to focus their interests, targeting specific departments and areas of study and beginning to work with faculty in these programs. For example, developmental faculty can help students to identify areas of college-level study in which they are interested and to work with these programs' faculty to ensure a successful transition from developmental to college-level work.

Faculty assignments can be made that move faculty between the collegiate world and the developmental world of the institution. The organizational structure can be reviewed in light of the need to treat developmental and remedial students not as patients in a hospital with the diagnosed disease of academic deficiency, but as individuals eager to make cognitive and intellectual gains. This focus on what students wish to accomplish academically rather than on what they lack in skills can justify housing developmental and remedial programs with other academic programs.

Community-based education, vocational training, or noncredit work can be tied to collegiate work in a similar fashion. Noncredit students can be encouraged to pursue instruction for credit. Cultural or other community programs can be tied to academic departments. And work with nontraditional students who are highly likely to begin with noncredit courses can include incentives to shift to credit courses and collegiate goals.

Structural Change and the Collegiate Role

The thesis of this book is that the community college should establish the collegiate function as its dominant educational role. However, community college educators may not wish to establish a collegiate community college by using the practices and policies that have been discussed thus far, and the critics may be correct in claiming that the community colleges as they are currently structured cannot provide effective collegiate education. There is another alternative. The community college can consider structural changes — including changing their educational role and changing their relationship with both college-preparatory and four-year schools — in an effort to build a dominant collegiate function. No other society has attempted to combine collegiate and technical education in a single two-year institution. Perhaps this calls for some reflection.

Two quite different structural changes for the community college could have a dramatic impact on the collegiate function: the establishment of transition schools and a public policy decision to make the community college the presumptive deliverer of all lower-division undergraduate education for the country. Two other structural changes have also been discussed in the literature: creating a four-year community college and locating all community colleges within university systems made up of two- and four-year schools.

Transition Schools

One alternative to asking the community college to provide both access and a successful collegiate function is to pursue a dominant collegiate function while at the same time removing a good deal of the developmental and remedial responsibility from the community college. Constricting the developmental role to only modest remediation support, as suggested above, leaves the community college with the responsibility of offering alternatives that meet the needs of those with serious developmental challenges.

Transition schools — centers of precollege instruction in reading, writing, and mathematics outside the community college — are one alternative. They could ensure college-preparedness for all students entering higher education, whether they enroll in a community college or a four-year school (Eaton, 1991). Adults as well as recent high school graduates could attend. These schools, by removing much of the responsibility for developmental and remedial education from the community college, would accomplish two goals. First, they would free community colleges to function primarily as sites of college-level study. Students would greatly benefit from an educational environment that was primarily focused on collegiate work. Second, they would be a potentially more effective way to offer precollegiate study and would prepare students for college-level work better than the community college.

Transition schools would not be a substitute for effective elementary and secondary education. They would be specialized educational centers established in local communities with a single purpose: to ensure that all students seeking enrollment in a college or university would possess the needed skills to do college-level work. These schools would teach reading, writing, and mathematics to young people and adults seeking to enter a community college who demonstrate that they are not yet able to undertake collegiate studies but who have the skills that will enable them to become college-ready. They would function as precollege centers.

Transition schools would replace many of the developmental and remedial efforts of the community college and four-year schools with the exception of developmental work for those with only mild educational deficiencies. They could be financed at least in part by reallocating funds that are already being used for this purpose in collegiate institutions and would require public oversight independent of local school districts and higher education institutions. There would be no charge to students who enroll. A transition school would have to document that students could undertake college-level work prior to their matriculation to a community college or four-year institution.

Transition schools would have several advantages. They would enhance access through providing a subsidized second chance for both young people and adults to develop needed skills for collegiate work. They could also overcome the limitations of elementary and secondary education more effectively than current higher education efforts. Colleges and universities do not do a particularly good job with developmental and remedial work. They are not funded for this purpose and therefore it is an inappropriate use of taxpayer subsidies. Transition schools can, on a temporary basis, overcome some of the limitations students suffer as a result of elementary and secondary school problems that cannot be solved easily or quickly.

Transition schools also would have several disadvantages. They are redundant. They are a stopgap measure and do not deal with the larger problems of national education. Because they would require demonstration of minimum cognitive competencies, they would be sorting environments, a situation that usually carries negative perceptions. They would probably not be fully funded through diversion of higher education resources used for developmental and remedial purposes and thus would call for more money, and they would cause disruption in community colleges because they could lead to staffing reductions.

However, as an aid to a dominant collegiate function, transition schools would ensure that students were ready to move into college-level work. This would allow the collegiate community college to focus more intently on the delivery of college-level learning and the creation of a campus environment in which students were highly motivated to adopt and pursue long-range educational goals. Transition schools would free up community colleges to devote their remaining developmental education programs to the students with whom they are the most successful. They are essential to the community college's responsible handling of additional restrictions on access.

Community Colleges That Deliver Only Lower-Division Work

With the unpleasant financial picture that faced the nation and higher education during the late 1980s and the early 1990s, some thought was given to making more extensive use of the community college, especially as a means to achieving the baccalaureate degree. One strategy to more fully utilize the community college would be to concentrate all lower-division undergraduate education there, removing it from four-year institutions. This effort, if it could be made cost-effective and acceptable to four-year institutions, would greatly strengthen the collegiate function of the community college.

Expanding the two-year institution to assume responsibility for all lower-division work would radically change the mission of the community college by rendering the collegiate function so prominent that other community college purposes would likely be eclipsed. The horizontal function of the community college would be diminished and its vertical function expanded. The community-based institution that was sought by Gleazer (1980) would give way to a more traditional, highly structured collegiate environment and Parnell's (1985b) vision of vocationalism would have to be adapted to college-level studies. Cohen and Brawer's (1987) commitment to collegiate education could provide much of the conceptual foundation for reframing the community college's mission.

Assuming responsibility for all lower-division work would significantly increase the transferable liberal arts and career education programs in the community college, resulting in a more collegiate culture. This would have an impact on academic standards, with community colleges and four-year schools working closely to establish performance expectations. It would also put community colleges in a powerful position to influence undergraduate education in the country because they would determine the foundation for all beginning baccalaureate studies. Curiously, in spite of the enormous numbers of students who begin their collegiate education in the community college, the two-year institution has had little effect on the shape and substance of the undergraduate curriculum across the country.

If community colleges delivered all lower-division education, their commitment to access would be even more important. To date, they have shared this responsibility with other educational institutions. While it can be argued that community colleges are the most important access point to higher education, they are not now the unique access point. If they were, their responsibility for educational preparedness, participation of minorities, and education of lower-income students would take on a heightened significance. This could strengthen the public policy commitment to community colleges and, more importantly, the financial commitment of states and the federal government.

Financially, expansion of the community college in this manner is equivocal. On one hand, considering the community college as the presumptive deliverer of lower-division education has been driven by efforts to reduce the price of higher education to students and the cost of higher education to the public. The comparatively low cost per full-time equivalent (FTE) student is the primary reason for community colleges to take on this role. On the other hand, although taxpayer support for community college FTEs is lower than support for students in four-year schools, no data are available that compare community college costs and costs for *only* lower-division study in a four-year setting. At present, the claim that community college expenditures per student cost the taxpayer less is based upon a comparison with a cost per student that assumes the additional expenses of a four-year operation. Expenditure per student in lower-division education may be less than expenditure per student over four years. Sorting out the levels of financial support needs to be handled carefully.

Assuming lower-division responsibility would change the relationship of the community college to the four-year world. Transfer and articulation issues would be central to both sectors. Faculty at two- and four-year institutions would be required to work closely together, and efforts to build an academic community across institutions would be essential. Two- and four-year faculty would be required to collaborate on curricular and pedagogical issues and academic standards. This would call for a major commitment by faculty to review curriculum and performance expectations across institutions, admissions practices that cut across institutions, and the state's policy about financing the transition from two- to four-year institutions.

Four-Year Community Colleges

Arguments that the community college should be something other than a two-year, autonomous institution are not new. Why raise them again here in connection with establishing a dominant collegiate function? First, it is worth considering that attempts to change institutional practice and policy, no matter how vigorous they are, may not produce a successful collegiate function. Second, the emergence of the two-year, autonomous institution as the most common community college structure is, as with most things, the result of historical accident and thus need not be considered sacred. Third, the evidence that the community college's collegiate effectiveness is less than it might be — coupled with the importance of community colleges as sites of educational opportunity — makes it reasonable to consider all major avenues of change to improve this situation. Fourth, structural change has been considered as a means of strengthening the community college or clarifying its mission mainly by its critics. Perhaps its friends should give this topic some thought. Finally, in the early 1990s, a small but significant number of states are discussing structural change for their community colleges. Ohio, Connecticut, and Minnesota are seriously debating mergers of freestanding community colleges with other types of institutions, and Florida is considering whether to make some community colleges four-year institutions. Community colleges have little foundation on which to encourage or combat these efforts.

Dougherty (1991, 1992) has made the most recent case for structured reform of the community college, especially for establishing four-year community colleges. This concept, as Dougherty points out, was described by Zwerling (1976), who argued that restructuring collegiate schools was a way to deliver more egalitarian messages about education. Zwerling calls for eliminating the community college and replacing it with either open-admission programs in four-year schools or four-year community colleges.

Dougherty does not provide either a detailed profile of the four-year community college or specifics regarding the transformation of the two-year college that would have to take place, and he does not address the political, financial, public policy, and educational policy issues that require attention, including its impact on access, its organizational culture, and the relationship between four-year community colleges and other four-year institutions. Dougherty does describe the advantages and liabilities of this newly structured institution. Advantages center on a greater ease of transition to upper-division work because students would not have to navigate two cultures, lower-division preparation would be better, course credits and financial aid would better survive the shift from lower-division to upper-division status, and occupational credits might fare better in relation to acquisition of the baccalaureate degree.

Liabilities include the possibility that four-year community colleges would remain at the bottom of the higher education hierarchy, occupying the same low-status and low-prestige niche that is currently held by the two-year college. In addition, the transition would be expensive. In the long run, these new four-year institutions might want to establish graduate programs, thereby diminishing their focus on undergraduate teaching and learning. Four-year community colleges also would produce too many graduates for available jobs and would fail to adequately meet the needs of occupational students who were not seeking a baccalaureate degree. Higher education — including many two-year community colleges — would oppose this transformation.

Branch Campuses

Dougherty also discusses the desirability of transforming community colleges into university branch campuses. More than 100 two-year college campuses or institutes in eighteen states are affiliated with state universities. In Nevada, Alaska, Hawaii, and Kentucky, the public community colleges are part of state university systems (Cohen and Brawer, 1989). Dougherty argues that shifting community colleges to branch-campus status would ease transfer and keep from discouraging students from pursuing the baccalaureate degree. The comprehensive community college could function as part of an institution or system, retaining its horizontal function and its autonomy. At the institutional level, the University of the District of Columbia pursued this structure during the 1980s, but did not implement it.

At the system level, the incorporation of the two-year college could follow the pattern of City University of New York or the State University of New York, with two critical changes: the two-year college would be required to have a major focus on access to the baccalaureate and admission to the upper-division college would have to be guaranteed at the time of admission to the community college. The collegiate function of two-year colleges that are incorporated within four-year or university structures would become more effective because these institutions would be free to concentrate on traditional academic work and college-level studies, and because they could guarantee access to the baccalaureate.

Would Structural Change Create Improvements?

Three reasons can be forwarded to support structural change. First, structural change would strengthen the collegiate function in two-year schools. Second, learning gains for students would be enhanced through structural change. And third, structural change would produce fiscal efficiencies that are badly needed in the difficult economic times of the 1990s.

However appealing these reasons may initially appear, evidence to support them is, at least at this time, less than compelling. Little proof can be found that altering structure by eliminating the freestanding community college would strengthen the collegiate function. For example, no available comparisons exist of the strength of the collegiate function in states that have different structures for their community colleges. Some research confirms, however, that structural change would have a favorable impact, at least on baccalaureate-degree attainment. Orfield and Paul (1992) argue that structure does have an effect on baccalaureate-degree attainment and thus, for our purposes, on the collegiate function. They analyzed the structure of higher education and baccalaureate attainment in five states — California, Indiana, Illinois, Florida, and Wisconsin. Their major finding is that states with the least reliance on community colleges have higher baccalaureate-degree attainment while those that rely more heavily on community colleges have lower baccalaureate-degree attainment (Orfield and Paul, 1992, p. 88). They claim that "at present the only route to the bachelor's degree with a high probability of success is to begin at a baccalaureate campus" (p. 98). Secondarily, students do better when two-year institutions are placed on four-year campuses and when transfer programs are separated from vocational-technical or adult education programs. According to Orfield and Paul, "Where two year programs are an important segment of a state's higher vocational program, separate transfer education from vocational-technical and adult education was clearly preferable" (p. 91).

Evidence also shows variations among states in transfer rates, yet another element of the collegiate function (Cohen, 1992). These variations, however, cannot be ascribed only to differences in structure. Cohen examined transfer rates in California, Texas, and Illinois. Texas's transfer rate was 28.2 percent, California's was 20.8 percent, and Illinois's was 21.5 percent. While California and Illinois had similar rates, their higher education structures are very different: Illinois relies to some extent on upper-division schools that are designed to take transfer students, while California houses four-year institutions whose relationship to the community colleges is more complex. Both these states were part of Orfield and Paul's study. Texas, like Illinois, relies to some extent on upper-division colleges, but its transfer rate differs significantly from that of Illinois. Cohen's brief scrutiny of these states suggests that variables other than structure are at play here, including demographics, financing, state policy, and testing.

There is virtually no evidence that creating different structures has an impact on student learning gains. For example, the states in which community colleges are part of a system, such as Nevada and New York, have not been compared to those in which community colleges are freestanding, such as Pennsylvania or Illinois. Thus, placing the community college within a larger higher education complex would require an act of faith about the effects of this action on students.

More data would be needed to confirm that changing the structure of the community college would be cost-effective. Two points are important here. First, information to compare lower-division costs across institutions is not available, so it remains to be seen whether or not community colleges are less costly than other institutions. Second, even if community colleges are less costly, this may not be a desirable phenomenon. It is questionable public policy to place the students who are the least-prepared for collegiate work in the institutions that have the fewest resources to devote to them.

With regard to the four specific structural suggestions offered here, transition schools and community colleges that deliver all lower-division education have yet to be tried. Transition schools would solve some problems of student preparation in relation to a dominant collegiate function but would be severely challenged on several grounds, especially the extent to which they would be perceived to be destroying access. The community college as presumptive deliverer of all lower-division work would produce a powerful collegiate function and radically diminish other community college purposes. It is not clear that there would be financial benefits to taxpayers in making this move. Four-year community colleges may produce some continuity of programming at the collegiate level, but they also appear to be new packages for the existing tensions and difficulties of the collegiate function in a two-year setting. Experience to date indicates that using branch campuses as the prevailing structure for the community college will do little to aid the collegiate function.

Are any of these structural changes even feasible? The political obstacles to implementing any of them would be daunting. The autonomous two-year college has a constituency that would fight for its retention. The financial and governance changes would also be complex. Dealing with faculty tenure and collective bargaining would not be easy. As with most major public policy changes, these changes could take place only if key individuals worked toward their realization.

Nonetheless, exploring these structural notions is of value to community college educators and to higher education in general. Elements of these ideas may be useful at a later time, and it is fruitful to consider structural as well as programmatic or operational changes in the community college in attempting to strengthen the collegiate role of these institutions.

Summary

Building a dominant collegiate function will not be easy. As this chapter suggests, major changes in the operation of institutions, fundamental commitments to access, the associate degree, and general education would all have to be considered. Further, the argument that the community college is structurally unsuited as a vehicle for the collegiate function deserves serious attention. Evidence is beginning to emerge that the present structure of the community college may inhibit baccalaureate-degree attainment in some states. Evidence or no, some states are seriously considering major alterations in their higher education structures that would have the effect of placing the once freestanding community college within a larger higher education complex.

Chapter Eight

Collegiate Education and the Nation's Access Agenda

Thus far the community college and its commitment to the collegiate function have been examined according to internal criteria: Does it make educational good sense to retain and enhance this function? Is the collegiate function appropriate to the community college's mission? Can the community college sustain an effective collegiate function? These questions have been answered in the affirmative.

This chapter focuses on the external environment in which the collegiate community college would operate. In particular, it explores the responsibility of the collegiate community college to the national commitment to mass higher education — the access agenda.

Although this book has called for further restriction of access for the community college, this is not inconsistent with the demand that the community colleges play a leadership role in furthering the nation's access agenda. As discussed in Chapter Three, access restrictions may be geographic, financial, personal, or academic. The restrictions that have been asked for in relation to the collegiate community college are academic; the other forms are not affected. The collegiate community college will remain the pivotal access institution for higher education; its location, price, and convenience will ensure that it remains central to the nation's access agenda. Further, on the campus, the community college's teaching culture and attitudes of encouragement toward students will remain intact. All of these features argue for the collegiate community college to play a leading role in building a stronger commitment to access at a national level.

The collegiate community college can assume three responsibilities that will meaningfully contribute to the national commitment to access. First, it can be a national leader in lower-division undergraduate teaching, learning, and curriculum. Second, it can be a national leader in strengthening public policy commitment to access. And third, it can assume national responsibility for educational achievement among minorities. A fourth responsibility, that of leading the transition to effective collegiate education for nontraditional students, was discussed in Chapter Six.

The Nation's Commitment to an Access Agenda

The nation's commitment to access is neither official nor clear nor permanent. Higher education has been treated as an opportunity in society, not a right. While elementary and secondary education are compulsory and binding on both the taxpayer and the student, collegiate education is not. There have been some attempts to approach college attendance from this perspective, but they are not widespread. Some states—for example, Nevada and Louisiana—require colleges and university systems to admit graduates of the various school districts within the state; in general, however, instead of guaranteeing participation in higher education for those who chose to attend, government has worked to ensure that there are no obstacles to a collegiate experience. To the extent that it is successful, it claims to be committed to access.

To date, although much rhetoric has been devoted to open access, U.S. public policy can be most accurately described as a commitment to limited access. *Open access* is used here to refer to a fully available system of higher education in which everyone who wishes to attend can do so. *Limited access* refers to placing restrictions on college attendance that can result in someone who wishes to attend college being prevented from doing so.

Among all higher education institutions, community colleges house the least restrictive access practices. This does not mean that they are totally accessible. As discussed in Chapter Seven, even the community college limits access. Nonetheless, more than one-half of all first-year college students are enrolled in community colleges and more than 40 percent of all higher education enrollments are in community colleges. This level of participation has been achieved not only through admission requirements that are more lenient than those of other institutions; additionally, once they are enrolled, students are not immediately penalized for failure through traditional probation or expulsion procedures. Instead, they are encouraged to keep on trying through strategies such as deferred grading, nonpenalty repetition of courses, and special studies. In the four-year sector, only the City University of New York's open-admission experiment in the 1970s is comparable.

Access is sometimes equated with *open admissions,* a phrase that has a variety of meanings. In the community college sector, it refers to institutional admission practices that allow students to enroll regardless of their competence to handle college-level work or their previous educational experiences. In its least restrictive form, open-admission practices provide an opportunity for any adult to enroll who is capable of "profiting from instruction." A high school diploma or its equivalent, the General Education Diploma (GED), is not essential, nor is the demonstrated competence to complete a community college curriculum.

In the four-year sector, schools are grouped according to whether their admissions are open, liberal, traditional, selective, or highly selective. The highly selective institutions have the most rigorous entrance requirements. At the other end of the continuum, 205 four-year institutions, or approximately 12 percent, are open in that they accept all high school graduates on a space-available basis and with the lowest of Scholastic Aptitude Test or American College Testing scores of all four-year institutions (Andersen, C., personal communication, April 9, 1992). The open-admission four-year institution has more demanding entrance requirements than the typical community college.

Public policy attention to access is grounded in the Servicemen's Readjustment Act of 1944 and the Higher Education

Act of 1965. The major theme on which policy on access has been constructed is the removal of obstacles to college attendance. At least five such obstacles have been the subject of public policy interest in access during the past thirty years: (1) limited finances to attend college, (2) inadequate academic preparation, (3) race and gender, (4) financial inability to attend higher-priced institutions, and (5) lack of motivation to attend college (Eaton, 1992a). Federal and state policies, practices, and projects have been focused on removing some or all of these obstacles. Community colleges have been the major beneficiaries of efforts to remove barriers caused by lack of finances or academic preparation.

How much access is enough? How many students should attend college before the country is satisfied that it is honoring its commitment to access? In an open-access scenario, where higher education is fully available, the answer to "How much access is enough?" is "As much as people want." Access is a response to consumer demand. In a limited-access scenario, one answer is "As much as people who can demonstrate minimum skill levels want." As defined here, limited access is access that requires some confirmation of college-readiness. A limited-access scenario might be limited based on other criteria, however, such as geography or financial means.

An open-access scenario would provide for full admission to all colleges and universities and full taxpayer subsidy for anyone attempting collegiate studies. This subsidy would be provided with the full understanding that some—perhaps even large—numbers of students might not be successful. Just as all students are required to attempt elementary and secondary education, all students would have the opportunity to attempt collegiate education. The public investment would be to bring as many students as possible within the higher education community and to accept very high attrition rates in the process of identifying those with sufficient competence to complete a degree.

A limited-access scenario would differ in two ways: it would emphasize the capability to succeed as a condition of entry to the higher education community and it would expect achievement levels with much lower attrition rates. A limited-access scenario would provide access only for those who are ready to take advantage of collegiate work. Participation in higher education would be contingent upon the academic preparation of each individual. This scenario, to be successful, cannot be used in conjunction with current secondary school preparation and testing strategies. Elementary and secondary education fail to prepare adequate numbers of students for collegiate work — especially racial minorities and low-income individuals. For limited access to be successful, the secondary school system would need reform or augmentation. This scenario would also require expansion and revision of strategies for documenting competencies to ensure that testing criteria are flexible enough and testing is done at frequent enough intervals to provide potential students with opportunities to demonstrate their readiness for college.

The Economic Foundation for an Access Agenda

A national commitment to access requires an economic foundation that is fiscally sound and that sustains adequate resources to support higher education. By the late 1980s and early 1990s, recessionary economic conditions resulted in neither of these conditions being met. The deteriorating economy had the effect of making higher education more costly for students, encouraging education on credit, and reducing the services that colleges and universities could provide. Although total higher education enrollments continued to grow during the initial years of the recession, the longer-range impact of these economic conditions, especially the potential for diminished access for lower-income students, was cause for concern. Further, the aggregate increases in enrollment masked problems that were emerging for some groups of students, especially black men.

Between 1977 and 1990, a decline in productivity, coupled with the financial policies of a Republican White House buttressed by an acquiescent Democratic Congress, resulted in a greater concentration of wealth among those who were already wealthy and a loss of real income among the less affluent. The average pretax earnings of the poorest 20 percent of Americans declined by 5 percent, while the most affluent 20 percent became 9 percent wealthier, before taxes (Reich, 1991). The middle class grew smaller, savings diminished, and investments declined. Internationalization of the economy and increases in immigration particularly affected low-skilled workers (Samuelson, 1992). More difficult economic times aggravated existing tensions and social problems: crime and violence increased and racism appeared to be on the rise. A society that was committed primarily to the welfare of the middle class would not or could not meet the needs of the poor and those with low incomes. At the same time, the cost of benefits to the middle class continued to increase as Medicare and Social Security payments escalated precipitously. All of this undermined the national sense that prosperity could solve all problems and was inevitable.

Even by 1990, it was difficult for many Americans to realize that the era of prosperity that had extended from the Second World War to the early 1970s had ended. Between 1945 and 1970, a growing Gross National Product, an expanding job market, a growing population, and baby boomers who were in need of services of all kinds produced an unprecedented era of economic expansion. It was in this environment that the community college reached its zenith in enrollment and influence. The growing economy made it acceptable to bring more and more individuals into an arena of comparative economic prosperity. One person's gain was not necessarily another's loss, and it was easier to be concerned about equity and social justice when the economic pie was expanding. It is not coincidental that the foundation for this country's greatest effort to date to deal with its most difficult and intractable social problem — racial inequality — was laid during this prosperous period.

Since the 1970s, economic growth has been more limited. Compared to the years immediately following World War II, growth in productivity slowed in both the 1970s and the 1980s and poverty increased in the 1980s ("A Better Yesterday," 1991). Between 1950 and 1970, the median family income rose 89 percent; since 1970, it has increased only 13 percent (Samuelson, 1992). Comparatively mild recessionary periods during the 1970s and the early 1980s gave way to a severe economic downturn in the late 1980s and early 1990s, which was characterized by a growing federal deficit, high unemployment, contraction of the major manufacturing industries, shrinkage of major service industries, a continuing unfavorable balance of trade, and a major erosion in competence and confidence in the nation's financial institutions. These declining revenues, coupled with an increased need for public services such as aiding the homeless, providing unemployment compensation, and combating poverty, drug usage, violence, and AIDS, stabilized or diminished public financing for all levels of education. A decline in prosperity also meant less interest in social justice and equity. Increasing racial violence, anti-Semitism, hostile reactions to newly arrived immigrants, sexism, and homophobia are unfortunately being seen.

Funding for American higher education has felt the impact of these restrictive economic conditions. Colleges and universities are in the worst financial position since World War II (Atwell, 1992). Between 1980 and 1990, total federal appropriations for education at all levels declined from $53.3 billion to $50.5 billion (in constant dollars) and federal appropriations for postsecondary education were stable at $26 billion (in constant dollars). In the early 1990s, state support for higher education declined. In fiscal year (FY) 1991, total state appropriations were $40.8 billion versus $40.1 billion in FY 1992. On average, approximately 7.4 percent of state budgets were provided for higher education in FY 1985, while 6.9 percent were allocated in FY 1990, (Ottinger, 1992). By the end of 1992, declining state appropriations, at least in seven states, were coupled with diminishing enrollments (American Council on Education, 1992). For community colleges, funding in constant dollars has decreased since FY 1987. Median expenditures were $4,270 in FY 1987 and $4,196 in FY 1990. Median revenue was $3,024 in 1987 and $2,821 in 1990 (American Association of Community and Junior Colleges, 1991).

Even greater than the concern for financing institutions has been the concern for financing students. During the 1980s, total student aid ($27.9 billion), adjusted for inflation, declined by almost 2 percent (Ottinger, 1992). Deteriorating economic conditions are producing higher and higher tuition, increased borrowing by students to finance their education, and changes in attendance patterns that result in students in higher socioeconomic groups attending less costly and less prestigious institutions and more students attending part-time. Although the evidence is minimal, those with the fewest resources may have ceased to pursue higher education at all. Low- and middle-income families have lost economic ground and median family income has declined slightly. These factors as well as a decline in per capita disposable income have undermined the ability of many to pay for college, especially for some low-income and minority students (Ottinger, 1992).

These financial conditions have also affected the community colleges. To date, the public cost per FTE in the community college is lower than in any other sector of higher education. In 1987–88, expenditure per student in four-year institutions was $15,535; in two-year institutions it was $4,974. Education and general expenses were $9,116 in four-year institutions and $4,590 in two-year schools (National Center for Education Statistics, 1991). There are no national data that compare expenditure per student in two-year colleges with lower-division expenditure per student in four-year colleges. In 1989–90, students in public and private two-year colleges received less financial aid through Title IV of the Higher Education Act, state programs, and institutional sources than students in public or private four-year institutions (American Association of Community and Junior Colleges, 1991).

Race and the Access Agenda

Although there were gains for minorities in higher education during the 1970s and 1980s, the early 1990s have become a time of considerable dissatisfaction with the levels of minority access, achievement, and influence and authority in higher education. The community college has been part of this dissatisfaction.

On one hand, educational circumstances for minorities have improved. Minority enrollments stood at 2.6 million in 1990. This was an all-time high in enrollments for all categories of minority students. In addition, in 1990, full-time higher education employment of minorities stood at 361,424 and showed increases in all categories. Employment of 58,935 full-time minority faculty and 17,450 minority administrators also reflected this trend (Carter and Wilson, 1992).

Minorities earned 70,456 associate degrees and 130,081 baccalaureate degrees in 1989. Minority master's degree recipients stood at 33,193 in 1989 with a slight decline for Native American men. Minorities earned 2,098 doctoral degrees in 1989 — a decrease since 1988 with a slight decline for black men and Hispanic men (Carter and Wilson, 1992). Minority achievement levels continued to indicate that various racial and ethnic groups did less well than the general student population or the white population. Again, some gains in achievement were seen, but they were not large enough to diminish the gaps in accomplishment that appeared related to race. The number of black men earning associate degrees was at its lowest point since 1985, and the number of black men and Native American men earning the bachelor's degree declined.

On the other hand, with the limited success in increasing the numbers and achievement of minority students has come increasing disenchantment with the strategies used to realize these goals. Affirmative action, the primary strategy for achieving minority goals, has engendered more and more skepticism and hostility. Whether it is used in admission practices or the hiring of faculty and administrators, affirmative action that includes racial preference has been increasingly criticized by whites and minorities alike.

Race has also been a key factor in producing the conflicts in the academic climate of the early 1990s. Debates on multiculturalism and political correctness have been in part the product of difficulty in coping with the changes that result from an expanded minority presence on college campuses. The range of approaches to the curriculum under the banner of multiculturalism has produced tension between those who seek a curriculum grounded in some vision of shared beliefs and those who focus on a curriculum of blame driven by rejection of the Western tradition and a preference for "minority only" studies. Minority students have been subject to racial hostility, while white students have claimed reverse discrimination.

Various racial and ethnic groups have sought to make gains through the interest-group approach characteristic of civil rights efforts since the 1960s. Racial politics on campus have been conducted through the interaction of various constituencies that have formed around race and gender, including student associations and faculty and administrative groups. This approach to minority participation and achievement was effective in establishing a beachhead for minorities in the 1970s and 1980s. In the 1990s, it has been met with increasing cynicism. Minorities have become yet another interest group making demands on limited resources but, in this era of declining resources, whites have also intensified their interest-group activities with the formation, for example, of white student groups in some campuses.

The Responsibilities of a Collegiate Community College

The community college has been the nation's most daring experiment in open higher education and a unique undertaking: no other country has been willing to open its colleges and universities to so many individuals with such a broad array of skills and academic backgrounds. The collegiate community college can be the finest expression of this experiment. And, in addition to its primary focus on its own educational role, it is uniquely positioned to assist in leading the nation's commitment to access.

The collegiate community college can provide leadership for the nation's access agenda in the areas of lower-division education, strengthening of the public policy commitment to access, and increasing educational achievement for minorities. The special features of the collegiate function allow it to play this role.

Leadership in Lower-Division Education

The collegiate community college is in a position to invest significant energy and talent in lower-division studies. Four-year institutions, in contrast, must devote time to the entire undergraduate curriculum as well as to graduate programs. Because of their freedom to concentrate on lower-division education, community colleges have an outstanding academic opportunity to explore key issues affecting curriculum, teaching, and assessment and to focus the applied scholarship interests of faculty.

The community college can establish itself by developing an agenda for academic leadership for lower-division undergraduate studies. Agenda items can include general education: the role of lower-division studies in the development of analytic and synthetic reasoning skills. They can include lower-division interdisciplinary education: models for interdisciplinary studies that provide advantages unavailable through traditional discipline-based introductory courses. The agenda should include a study of the associate degree–baccalaureate degree relationship—how the associate degree can be rendered more meaningful in structuring the lower-division experience. And, it can include transfer—the relationship between two- and four-year institutions as expressed through agreements about course content and academic standards.

The agenda that is developed needs to express pedagogy. Community college faculty are the most experienced in the world at dealing with underprepared students. How can this be of help to four-year institutions? The agenda should address multicultural curricula, asking whether or not the higher education enterprise can reposition and reshape curricular content to be truly meaningful as the country continues to undergo dramatic demographic changes.

These are only a few of the items that are important to an academic leadership agenda for lower-division education. Other items that are discipline-specific or based on career programs can be developed as well. The crucial point is that the community college needs to energetically provide leadership in the important area of the effectiveness of higher education.

The agenda can be carried out through vigorous leadership at the institutional, state, and national levels. Existing organizations such as the AACC and especially its affiliate councils such as the Council for Instructional Administrators and the Community College Humanities Association are essential for this agenda. Other academically based two-year organizations such as the Community College General Education Association or the Two-Year Chemical Society are extremely valuable. University centers that house doctoral programs in the community colleges are also a powerful resource in establishing and carrying out this agenda.

Influence on Public Policy About Access

The national commitment to access has been consistent since 1965, but it has not been strong enough. Access has been supported through rhetoric, federal student aid funding targeted to low-income and minority students, and special federal programs for the educationally underprepared. Having a commitment to access is only one national priority among others such as ensuring choice or enforcing academic standards. Access, for example, competes with choice in federal student aid funding. Grant and loan programs assist middle- and upper-middle-income students as much as low-income students, if not more (McPherson and Schapiro, 1991; Mortenson, 1990). This occurs when students of moderate means receive grants or loans that enable them to attend high-tuition institutions, reducing the funds available for low-income students to attend moderately priced institutions. The states provide another example, with more and more institutions raising admission requirements as a means of coping with reduced funding, thereby reducing access. These more demanding admission requirements are not accompanied by precollege support programs for low-income students, who are the most likely to be academically underprepared.

The collegiate community college needs to influence public policy to make access a top national priority for higher education. The structure is there to pursue this goal, through national organizations such as the AACC and the Association of Community College Trustees (ACCT), and through state and regional operations such as the state directors of community colleges and the ACCT regional divisions. Influencing public policy should be a two-part effort. At the federal level, it requires working with the higher education community and the government to structure student grant and loan programs so that access is the primary criterion and low-income students and first-generation college students receive priority attention. At the state level, it requires working with legislators to refashion institutional aid so that it provides primary support for the institutions that house the largest number of low-income students. It is the middle class who primarily benefits from federal student aid and from public subsidies provided to higher education at the state level. Access policy should be focused first and foremost on those for whom college would not be possible if it were not for federal and state support. To the extent that state and federal funds subsidize students who would be able to go to college anyway, they are not supporting access as a top priority.

Because community colleges enroll more of those students for whom access is of profound importance, such as lower-income and minority students and the academically underprepared, it is the best-suited of all higher education sectors to lead this public policy initiative. Its participation would be in the best interests of both the community college and the national commitment to access. Indeed, the absence of the community college from the forefront of leadership is both perplexing and dismaying.

There are many calls for improved funding for higher education at the state and federal levels. Some changes intended to improve access, such as the restructuring of Pell Grants, were made with the authorization of the 1992 Higher Education Act. To date, much less attention has been paid to a comprehensive restructuring of higher-education financing that would target access as the most critical goal. McPherson and Schapiro (1991) have offered the most thorough analysis of higher education financing, exploring ideas such as federalizing student aid to low-income students, increasing the "ability-to-pay" financing of educational costs, and reducing across-the-board subsidies provided by the states. The collegiate community college needs to understand these issues and, through suggestions for a comprehensive restructuring, more specific financial initiatives, or both, make the case for expanded public subsidies for access.

Community college leaders need to acknowledge, however, the possibility that this investment in access as a top priority may not pay off when students attend a community college, even one with a dominant collegiate function. Although, by any measures generally used, community colleges have lower expenditures per student, those expenditures may be too low to provide effective education. An investigation needs to be undertaken of whether current levels of support for the community college are adequate. Analysis of lower-division expenditures per student in two-year and four-year institutions may confirm that the community college is *not* a more cost-effective institution. It may not be advantageous for the taxpayer to subsidize the community college rather than a four-year college. As was noted in Chapter Five, a case can be made that the community college attracts students who do not succeed at college-level work, actually increasing the cost of education by forcing public subsidy of additional students under dubious circumstances. This does not invalidate the earlier point, however: given current funding levels, a dominant collegiate function would provide a more demanding educational experience for more students and better prepare them for either more education or work, at the lowest cost available.

Commitment to Racial Minorities

The collegiate community college, as has been noted, is an important factor in dealing with the challenges of race. The community college enrolls more minorities than any single sector of higher education — approximately 1.2 million students in 1990 (Carter and Wilson, 1992). Minorities made up 23 percent of enrollments in the 1,250 community colleges in Fall 1990. More black students (509,000) were enrolled in community colleges than in historically black colleges (207,547). In 1990, Hispanic enrollment stood at 414,000, while Asian enrollment (212,000) had grown significantly and Native American enrollment approached 54,000 (Carter and Wilson, 1992). By comparison, at approximately 2,250 four-year institutions, minority enrollment stood at 17 percent, or 1.4 million: 715,000 blacks, 364,000 Hispanics, 343,000 Asian Americans, and 48,000 Native Americans.

Although the community college has been a crucial access site for minorities, it has played an equivocal role in achievement for these groups. The educational attainment of blacks and Hispanics is neither as great as that of white students nor equal to that of the general student population (National Center for Education Statistics, 1991). Minorities do not complete degrees to the extent that they are represented in the community college population. In 1987, minorities received 17 percent of associate degrees although they constituted more than 20 percent of the community college population. Although the data are questionable, transfer rates also appear to be lower for minorities. Transfer rates for Hispanics (23 percent) and blacks (18 percent) who entered community colleges in 1980 were lower than those of white high school seniors; Asian Americans (41 percent) and Native Americans (30 percent) did better. Looking at the general picture, 18 percent of all high school seniors who began full-time study in a community college in 1980 received a baccalaureate within six years, while 45 percent of those who enrolled in four-year public colleges and 52 percent of those who enrolled in four-year independent colleges received the baccalaureate in six years (Carter, 1990). Although some question whether a connection ought to exist between the number of minority students participating in higher education and the number who obtain degrees or transfer, others point to these statistical differences as significant.

Given the extent to which minorities make use of the community college opportunity, these institutions can profit from paying additional attention to issues such as recruitment of minority faculty, achievement among minority students, and multiculturalism in the curriculum. Minority faculty have a limited presence in community colleges, as they do in higher education generally (National Center for Education Statistics, 1991). Community colleges have invested even less time in curricular change focused on multiculturalism than their four-year counterparts (Levine and Cureton, 1992). Some of these curricular changes are needed and would be of particular interest and value to minorities.

The minority students who attend community colleges are much more likely to have lower incomes than their counterparts in the four-year sector. Because of this situation and the extent to which minorities rely on the community college as their entry point to higher education, the community college's emphasis on achievement and access to the baccalaureate can have a powerful impact on the educational attainment of these students. If the community college does not invest in an effective collegiate function, minority students will be tracked away from baccalaureate education. The community college that does not have an effective collegiate function is performing the cooling-out function for minorities in the deleterious manner described by community college critics.

Summary

The collegiate community college is the nation's most important resource for strengthening the national commitment to access. The uneven history of policies toward access, the distressing economic conditions of the country, and the limited benefits that access policy has offered to minorities are all causes for concern.

While the collegiate community college alone will not resolve these problems, it can take certain steps to honor its responsibilities and strengthen its role in the national commitment to access. If the collegiate community college develops an intellectual tradition for lower-division education, it can establish an academic leadership agenda in that area. The collegiate community college remains the nation's pivotal access institution; therefore, it can more strongly influence policy discussions about access at both the federal and state levels. And because it offers more to minorities through emphasis on access to the baccalaureate, the collegiate community college enlarges and expands an achievement agenda for minorities that goes beyond earlier commitments to participation.

References

Adelman, C. *The Way We Are: The Community College as American Thermometer.* Washington, D.C.: U.S. Department of Education, Office of Educational Research and Improvement, Feb. 1992.

Alfred, R. L. "Positioning Alternatives and New Partnerships." In J. S. Eaton (ed.), *Colleges of Choice.* New York: Macmillan, 1988.

Alfred, R. L., and Linder, V. P. *Rhetoric to Reality: Effectiveness in Community Colleges.* Ann Arbor, Mich.: Community College Consortium, University of Michigan, 1990.

Alfred, R. L., Peterson, R. O., and White, T. H. *Making Community Colleges More Effective.* Ann Arbor, Mich.: Community College Consortium, University of Michigan, 1992.

American Association of Community and Junior Colleges. *Some Telling Facts About Two-Year Colleges.* Washington, D.C.: American Association of Community and Junior Colleges, 1986.

American Association of Community and Junior Colleges. *A Summary of Selected National Data Pertaining to Community, Technical, and Junior Colleges.* Washington, D.C.: American Association of Community and Junior Colleges, June 1991.

American Council on Education. *Bulletin,* Dec. 18, 1992.

Association of American Colleges. *Integrity in the College Curriculum: A Report to the College Community.* Washington, D.C.: Association of American Colleges, 1985.

Astin, A. W. *Minorities in American Higher Education: Recent Trends,*

Current Prospects, and Recommendations. San Francisco: Jossey-Bass, 1982.

Astin, A. W. "Strengthening Transfer Programs." In G. B. Vaughan and Associates, *Issues for Community College Leaders in a New Era.* San Francisco: Jossey-Bass, 1983.

Atwell, R. H. "Financial Prospects for Higher Education." The Higher Education Research Program sponsored by the Pew Charitable Trusts. *Policy Perspectives,* Sept. 1992, *4*(3), 5b–7b.

Barton, J. W. "Trends in the Junior College Curriculum." *The Junior College Journal,* May 1935, *5*(8), 405–418.

Bennett, W. J. *To Reclaim a Legacy: A Report on the Humanities in Higher Education.* Washington, D.C.: National Endowment for the Humanities, 1984.

"A Better Yesterday," Survey America. *The Economist,* Oct. 26, 1991, *321*(7730), 1–26.

Bogue, J. P. *The Community College.* New York: McGraw-Hill, 1950.

Boyer, E. L. *Scholarship Reconsidered: Priorities of the Professoriate.* Princeton, N.J.: Carnegie Foundation for the Advancement of Teaching, 1990.

Boylan, H. R., and Bonham, B. S. "The Impact of Developmental Programs." *Review of Research in Developmental Education,* 1992, *9*(5), Boone, N.C.: Appalachian State University.

Breneman, D., and Nelson, S. *Financing Community Colleges: An Economic Perspective.* Washington, D.C.: The Brookings Institution, 1981.

Brick, M. *Forum and Focus for the Junior College Movement: The American Association of Junior Colleges.* New York: Teachers College Press, 1964.

Brint, S., and Karabel, J. *The Diverted Dream: Community Colleges and the Promise of Educational Opportunity in America 1900–1985.* New York: Oxford University Press, 1989.

Campbell, D. S. *A Critical Study of the Stated Purposes of the Junior College.* Contribution to Education no. 70. Nashville, Tenn.: George Peabody College for Teachers, 1930.

Campbell, D. S. "The Junior College Curriculum." *The Junior College Journal,* Nov. 1932, *3*(2), 63–64.

Campbell, D. S. "The Junior College Curriculum." *The Junior College Journal,* May 1933, *3*(8), 416–419.

Carter, D. J. "Community and Junior Colleges: A Recent Profile." *Research Briefs,* Washington, D.C.: American Council on Education, 1990, *4*(1).

Carter, D. J., and Wilson, R. W. *Tenth Annual Status Report on Minorities in Higher Education.* Washington, D.C.: American Council on Education, Jan. 1992.

Cheney, L. V. *Tyrannical Machine: A Report on Educational Practices and What Has Gone Wrong and Our Best Hopes for Setting Them Right.* Washington, D.C.: National Endowment for the Humanities, 1990.

Clark, B. R. "The Cooling-Out Function in Higher Education." *American Journal of Sociology,* 1960a, *65*(6), 569–576.

Clark, B. R. *The Open Door College: A Case Study.* New York: McGraw-Hill, 1960b.

Clark, B. R. "The 'Cooling-Out' Function Revisited." In G. B. Vaughan, *Questioning the Community College Role.* New Directions for Community Colleges, no. 32. San Francisco: Jossey-Bass, 1980.

Clowes, D. A., and Levin, B. H. "Community, Technical, and Junior Colleges: Are They Leaving Higher Education?" *Journal of Higher Education,* May–June 1989, *60*(3), 349–355.

Cohen, A. M. *Dateline '79: Heretical Concepts for the Community College.* Beverly Hills, Calif.: Glenco, 1969.

Cohen, A. M. "Dateline '79 Revisited." In G. B. Vaughan, *Questioning the Community College Role.* New Directions for Community Colleges, no. 32. San Francisco: Jossey-Bass, 1980.

Cohen, A. M. "Leading the Educational Program." In G. B. Vaughan and Associates, *Issues for Community College Leaders in a New Era.* San Francisco: Jossey-Bass, 1983.

Cohen, A. M. "Associate Degree Prevailing." *Community, Technical, and Junior College Journal,* Dec.–Jan. 1985–1986, *56*(3), 24–27.

Cohen, A. M. "Degree Achievement by Minorities in Community Colleges." *The Review of Higher Education,* Summer 1988, *2*(4), 383–402.

Cohen, A. M. "Tracking the Transfers: State Policy and Practice." *Transfer,* Oct. 1992, *3*(7), Washington, D.C.: National Center for Academic Achievement and Transfer, American Council on Education.

Cohen, A. M., and Associates. *A Constant Variable.* San Francisco: Jossey-Bass, 1971.

Cohen, A. M. and Brawer, F. B. *The Two-Year College Instructor Today.* New York: Praeger, 1977.

Cohen, A. M., and Brawer, F. B. *The Collegiate Function of Community Colleges: Fostering Higher Learning Through Curriculum and Student Transfer.* San Francisco: Jossey-Bass, 1987.

Cohen, A. M., and Brawer, F. B. *The American Community College.* (2nd ed.) San Francisco: Jossey-Bass, 1989.

Cohen, A. M., and Ignash, J. "Total Community College Curriculum Study 1991." In *Probing the Community College Transfer Function.* Washington, D.C.: National Center for Academic Achievement and Transfer, American Council on Education, 1993.

Colvert, C. C. "A Half Century of Junior Colleges." *The Junior College Journal,* 1947, *17*(6), 244–247.

Cross, K. P. *The Junior College Student: A Research Description.* Princeton, N.J.: Educational Testing Service, 1968.

Cross, K. P. "Community Colleges on the Plateau." *Journal of Higher Education,* Mar.–Apr. 1981, *52*(2), 113–123.

Cross, K. P. "Thirty Years Have Passed: Trends in General Education." In B. L. Johnson (ed.), *General Education in Two-Year Colleges.* New Directions for Community Colleges, no. 40. San Francisco: Jossey-Bass, 1982.

Cross, K. P. "The Underside of the Push for Degrees." The Higher Education Research Program sponsored by the Pew Charitable Trusts. *Policy Perspectives,* Apr. 1990, *3*(2), 1–2.

Diener, T. *Growth of an American Invention: A Documentary History of the Junior and Community College Movement.* Westport, Conn.: Greenwood Press, 1986.

Dougherty, K. J. "The Effects of Community Colleges: Aid or Hindrance to Socioeconomic Attainment?" *Sociology of Education,* 1987, *60,* 86–103.

Dougherty, K. J. "The Politics of Community College Expansion: Beyond the Functionalist and Class-Reproduction Explanations." *American Journal of Education,* May 1988, pp. 351–393.

Dougherty, K. J. "The Community College at the Crossroads:

The Need for Structured Reform." *Harvard Educational Review,* Aug. 1991, *61*(3), 311–336.

Dougherty, K. J. "Community Colleges and Baccalaureate Attainment." *Journal of Higher Education,* Mar.–Apr. 1992, *63*(2), 188–214.

Eaton, J. S. (ed.). *Colleges of Choice: The Enabling Impact of the Community College.* New York: Macmillan, 1988.

Eaton, J. S. "A Perspective on the Future of Community Colleges." *Management Issues,* May 1990, Washington, D.C.: KPMG Peat Marwick.

Eaton, J. S. *The Unfinished Agenda: Higher Education and the 1980s.* New York: Macmillan, 1991.

Eaton, J. S. "The Evaluation of Access Policy: 1965–1990." In *American Higher Education: Purposes, Problems and Public Perceptions.* Queentown, Md.: The Aspen Institute, 1992a.

Eaton, J. S. (ed.). *Financing Nontraditional Students: A Seminar Report.* Washington, D.C.: American Council on Education, 1992b.

Eaton, J. S. "Presidents and Curriculum." *Transfer,* Nov. 1992c, *3*(8), Washington, D.C.: The National Center for Academic Achievement and Transfer, American Council on Education.

Eells, W. C. *The Junior College.* Boston: Houghton Mifflin, 1931a.

Eells, W. C. "What Manner of Child Shall This Be?" *The Junior College Journal,* Feb. 1931b, *1*(5), 309–328.

Eells, W. C. *Present Status of Junior College Terminal Education.* Washington, D.C.: American Association of Junior Colleges, 1941.

El-Khawas, E. *Campus Trends.* Washington, D.C.: American Council on Education, 1992.

El-Khawas, E., Carter, D., and Ottinger, C. *Community College Fact Book.* New York: Macmillan, 1988.

Frye, J. H. *The Vision of the Public Junior College, 1900–1940: Professional Goals and Popular Aspirations.* New York: Greenwood Press, 1992.

Gleazer, E. J. "Analysis of Junior College Growth." *The Junior College Journal,* Feb. 1959, *29*(6), 354–360.

Gleazer, E. J. *This Is the Community College.* Boston: Houghton-Mifflin, 1968.

Gleazer, E. J. "Community Colleges: The Decade Ahead." Paper presented to Florida Association of Community Colleges, Miami, Fla., Nov. 1, 1979. (ED 188 660)

Gleazer, E. J. *The Community College: Values, Vision, Vitality.* Washington, D.C.: American Association of Community and Junior Colleges, 1980.

Green, M. *The American College President.* Washington, D.C.: American Council on Education, 1986.

Grubb, W. N. "The Bandwagon One More: Vocational Preparation for High-Tech Occupations." *Harvard Educational Review,* 1984, *54*(4), 429–451.

Grubb, W. N. "Vocationalizing Higher Education: The Causes of Enrollment and Completion in Public Two-Year Colleges 1970–1980." *Economics of Education Review,* 1988, *7*(3), 301–319.

Grubb, W. N. "The Effects of Differentiation in Educational Attainment: The Case of Community Colleges." *The Review of Higher Education,* Summer 1989, *12*(4), 349–374.

Grubb, W. N. "The Decline of Transfer Rates: Evidence from National Longitudinal Surveys." *Journal of Higher Education,* Mar.–Apr. 1991, *62*(2), 194–217.

Grubb, W. N. "Correcting Conventional Wisdom: Community College Impact on Students' Jobs and Salaries." *Community, Technical, and Junior College Journal,* June–July 1992, *62*(6), 10–14.

Higher Education for American Democracy. Vol. 1: *Establishing the Goals.* Washington, D.C.: U.S. Government Printing Office, 1947.

Hillmer, M. A. "Terminal Curriculum Offered in Public Junior Colleges in the United States." *The Junior College Journal,* Nov. 1949, *20*(3), 128–130.

Hillway, T. *The American Two-Year College.* New York: Harper-Collins, 1958.

Jencks, C., and Riesman, D. *The Academic Revolution.* New York: Doubleday, 1968.

Johnson, B. L. *General Education in Action.* Washington, D.C.: American Council on Education, 1952.

Johnson, B. L. (ed.). *General Education in Two-Year Colleges.* New Directions for Community Colleges, no. 40. San Francisco: Jossey-Bass, 1982.

Karabel, J. "Community Colleges and Social Stratification." *Harvard Educational Review,* Nov. 1972, *42*(4), 521–562.

Karabel, J. "Protecting the Portals: Class and the Community College." *Social Policy,* May–June 1974, *5,* 12–18.

Karabel, J. "Community Colleges and Social Stratification in the 1980s." In L. S. Zwerling (ed.), *The Community College and Its Citizens.* New Directions for Community Colleges, no. 54. San Francisco: Jossey-Bass, 1986.

Koltai, L. "General Education and the Transfer Function." In B. L. Johnson (ed.), *General Education in Two-Year Colleges.* New Directions for Community Colleges, no. 40. San Francisco: Jossey-Bass, 1982.

Koos, L. V. *The Junior College Movement.* Boston: Ginn, 1925.

Lange, A. F. "The Junior College — What Manner of Child Shall This Be?" *School and Society,* 1918, *7,* 211–216.

Lee, V. L., Mackie, C. J., and Marks, H. M. "Persistence to the Baccalaureate Degree for Students Who Transfer from Community College." Presentation to American Educational Research Assciation, San Francisco, Calif., Apr. 1992.

Levine, A., and Cureton, J. "The Quiet Revolution: Eleven Facts about Multiculturalism and the Curriculum." *Change,* Jan.–Feb. 1992, *24*(1), 25–29.

Lombardi, J. F. *Resurgence of Occupational Education.* Topical Paper no. 65. Los Angeles: University of California, Los Angeles, ERIC-Junior Colleges, 1978.

Lombardi, J. F. *The Decline of Transfer Education.* Los Angeles: University of California, Los Angeles, ERIC-Junior Colleges, 1979.

Lombardi, J. F. "What's Happened to the Associate Degree?" *Eric Junior College Resource Review.* Los Angeles: University of California, Los Angeles, ERIC-Junior Colleges, May 1980, pp. 1–4.

McDowell, F. M. *The Junior College.* Bulletin no. 35. Washington, D.C.: Department of the Interior, Bureau of Education, U.S. Government Printing Office, 1919.

McGrath, D., and Spear, M. B. *The Academic Crisis of the Community College.* Albany: State University of New York, 1991.

McPherson, M. S., and Schapiro, M. O. *Keeping College Affordable.* Washington, D.C.: The Brookings Institution, 1991.

Mahoney, J. "Memorandum to James F. Gollattscheck." Washington, D.C.: American Association of Community and Junior Colleges, January 18, 1990.

Monroe, C. R. *Profile of the Community College*. San Francisco: Jossey-Bass, 1972.

Mortenson, T. G. *The Reallocation of Financial Aid from Poor to Middle Income and Affluent Students 1978–1990*. ACT Student Financial Aid Research Report Series, May 1990, 90–92. Iowa City, Iowa: American College Testing.

National Center for Education Statistics. *Digest of Education Statistics, 1991*. Washington, D.C.: U.S. Department of Education, Office of Educational Research and Improvement, National Center for Education Statistics, 1991. (NCES 91-697)

Orfield, G., and Paul, F. G. "State Higher Education Systems and College Completion." Final Report to The Ford Foundation, Nov. 1992.

Ottinger, C. A. *1984–85 Fact Book in Higher Education*. New York: Macmillan, 1984.

Ottinger, C. A. "College Graduates in the Labor Market: Today and the Future." *Research Briefs*, Washington, D.C.: American Council on Education, 1990, *1*(5).

Ottinger, C. A. "Economic Trends and Higher Education." *Research Briefs*, Washington, D.C.: American Council on Education, 1992, *3*(2).

Palmer, J. C. "The Scholarly Activity of Community College Faculty: Findings of a National Survey." In J. C. Palmer and G. B. Vaughan (eds.), *Fostering a Climate for Faculty Scholarship at Community Colleges*. Washington, D.C.: American Association of Community and Junior Colleges, 1992.

Palmer, J. C. "Faculty Practices and Attitudes as Teachers and Scholars: A Review of Research." In G. A. Baker, J. Dudziak, and P. Tyler (eds.), *A Handbook on the American Community College*. Westport, Conn.: Greenwood Press, 1994.

✴ Palmer, J. C., and Eaton, J. S. *Setting the National Agenda: Academic Achievement and Transfer*. Washington, D.C.: National Center for Academic Achievement and Transfer, American Council on Education, 1991.

Palmer, J. C., and Pugh, M. "The Community College Contribution to the Education of Bachelor's Degree Graduates:

A Case Study in Virginia." In *Probing the Community College Transfer Function.* Washington, D.C.: National Center for Academic Achievement and Transfer, American Council on Education, 1993.

Palmer, J. C., and Vaughan, G. B. (eds.). *Fostering a Climate for Faculty Scholarship at Community Colleges.* Washington, D.C.: American Association of Community and Junior Colleges, 1992.

Parnell, D. "President Dale Parnell: An Interview." *The Community and Junior College Journal,* Sept. 1981, *52*(1), 3–5.

Parnell, D. (ed.). *Associate Degree Preferred.* Washington, D.C.: American Association of Community and Junior Colleges, 1985a.

Parnell, D. *The Neglected Majority.* Washington, D.C.: American Association of Community and Junior colleges, 1985b.

Parnell, D. "Why Applied Academics?" *The Community, Technical, and Junior College Times,* July 17, 1990, *2*(15), 2.

Parnell, D. "What Is the Associate Degree Worth?" *The Community, Technical, and Junior College Times,* Jan. 1, 1991, *3*(1), 2, 8.

Pascarella, E. T., and Terenzini, P. T. *How College Affects Students.* San Francisco: Jossey-Bass, 1991.

Pincus, F. L. "Tracking in Community Colleges." *Insurgent Sociologist,* 1974, *4*, 17–35.

Pincus, F. L. "The False Promises of Community Colleges: Class Conflict and Vocational Education." *Harvard Educational Review,* 1980, *50*(3), 332–361.

Raisman, N. *Directing General Education Outcomes.* New Directions for Community Colleges, no. 81. San Francisco: Jossey-Bass, 1993.

Ravitch, D. "Multiculturalism: E Pluribus Plures." *American Scholar,* Summer 1990, pp. 332–354.

Reich, R. B. *The Work of Nations.* New York: Vintage, 1991.

Richardson, R. C., Fisk, E. C., and Okun, M. A. *Literacy in the Open-Access College.* San Francisco: Jossey-Bass, 1983.

Samuelson, R. J. "How Our American Dream Unraveled." *Newsweek,* Mar. 2, 1992, *119*(9), 32–39.

Schlesinger, A. *The Disuniting of America.* New York: W. W. Norton, 1992.

Seashore, C. E. *The Junior College Movement.* Troy, Mo.: Holt, Rinehart & Winston, 1940.

Seidman, E. *In the Words of the Faculty: Perspectives on Improving Teaching and Educational Quality in Community Colleges.* San Francisco: Jossey-Bass, 1985.

Study Group on the Condition of Excellence in American Higher Education. *Involvement in Learning: Realizing the Potential of American Higher Education.* Washington, D.C.: U.S. Department of Education, National Institute of Education, 1984.

Taylor, A. S. "Curricular Research Is Urgently Needed." *The Junior College Journal,* Feb. 1933, *3*(5), 246–248.

Thomas, F. W. "The Functions of the Junior College." In W. M. Proctor (ed.), *The Junior College: Its Organization and Administration.* Stanford, Calif.: Stanford University Press, 1927.

Thornton, J. W. *The Community Junior College.* New York: Wiley, 1960.

Thurow, L. Presentation to Business–Higher Education Forum, American Council on Education. Tucson, Ariz., Feb. 1, 1992.

Vaughan, G. B. (ed.). *Questioning the Community College Role.* New Directions for Community Colleges, no. 32. San Francisco: Jossey-Bass, 1980.

Vaughan, G. B. "Scholarship in Community Colleges: Path to Respect." *Educational Record,* Spring 1988, *69*(2), 26–31.

Vaughan, G. B., and Palmer, J. C. (eds.). *Enhancing Teaching and Administration Through Scholarship.* New Directions for Community Colleges. San Francisco: Jossey-Bass, 1991.

Weersing, F. J. "Misconceptions Regarding the Junior College." *The Junior College Journal,* Mar. 1931, *1*(6), 363–369.

Zook, G. F. "The Past Twenty Years – The Next Twenty Years." *The Junior College Journal,* 1940, *10*(9), 617–623.

Zwerling, L. S. *Second Best: The Crisis of the Community College.* New York: McGraw-Hill, 1976.

Zwerling, L. S. *The Community College and Its Critics.* New Directions for Community Colleges, no. 54. San Francisco: Jossey-Bass, 1986.

Index

A